A Dropped Glove in Regent Street

Christmas 2001,
Love always
Pat.

A Dropped Glove in Regent Street

An Autobiography by Other Means

Don Coles

FOREWORD BY
Alberto Manguel

Published with the generous assistance of The Canada Council for the
Arts and the Book Publishing Industry Development Program of the
Department of Canadian Heritage.

Signal Editions is an imprint of Véhicule Press
Signal Editions editor: Carmine Starnino

Cover design: David Drummond

Photograph (frontispiece) of the author by Danielle Schaub
Set in Adobe Minion and Futura by Simon Garamond
Printed by Marquis Printing Inc.

LIBRARY AND ARCHIVES CANADA CATALOGUING IN PUBLICATION
Coles, Don
A dropped glove in Regent Street : an autobiography
by other means / Don Coles
ISBN 1-55065-222-2
I. Title.
PS8555.O439Z463 2007   C814'.54   C2007-900559-4

Signal Editions is an imprint of Véhicule Press.

Published by Véhicule Press, Montréal, Québec, Canada
www.vehiculepress.com

Distribution in Canada: LitDistCo

Distribution USA: Independent Publishers Group

Printed in Canada on 100% post-consumer recycled paper.

*To anyone who finds herself, himself, in these pages,
I'll hope that the discovery comes with some degree
of pleasure. It was good remembering you.
Well, most of you.*

Contents

Foreword

Alberto Manguel

AT THE END of his long poem *Little Bird*, subtitled "A Last Letter to My Father", Don Coles reflects that absence forces us to acknowledge our own existence, not through awareness of our physical condition but through what we say or have said, "by our lives' casual talk." The noises we make as we pass through life somehow reassures us, like whistling in the dark. We speak to know that we are here.

Mainly through poetry, but also in his novel, *Doctor Bloom's Story*, and now with the remarkable prose collected in *A Dropped Glove in Regent Street,* Coles has been making his own brand of illuminating and self-defining "casual talk" for several decades now. The term, however, is deceiving. Casual it may well be, in the sense of informal, produced by chance; but then, (Shelley *dixit*) neither we nor our words are exempt "From chance, and death, and mutability." It is under these terrible three that we make our "casual talk" and, in this light, it is a miracle that there should be any talk at all, and even more the kind of talk in which Coles so brightly excels.

The nonchalant tone and breeziness of his observations make it easy for us to forget their originality and keen intelligence. To tell us, after reading a biography of Diderot, that a writer's brilliant observations of a place or a situation do not require the proper experience of being in that place or that situation, and that he (Coles) would "settle" for that "sort of 'seeing' anytime," is bravely to admit that facts are not everything they're made up to be, and that the reality of thoughtful intuition takes precedence (for an artist) over the reality of the physical senses. To note that "memory's great gift" consists in persuading us that the faces of those we've lost "*haven't* gone," and then to observe, as an afterthought, that "they may even add up to the phenomena of love," has the carelessness of true wisdom.

"I'm not forgetful of the fact," Coles confesses, "that in the act of

9

writing I often tap into images, thoughts, insights, arrangements, scenes, which are well *beyond* my normal everyday images and thoughts. Many such, and many more forays into places and events that my life has never come close to, that some might feel I haven't earned the right to speak of, where I'm riding solely on my imagination and depending on that to make up in originality and vividness for the absence of personally-observed detail." Hidden in this *confessio propria infirmitatis* is a definition of the writer's craft.

And yet, "personally-observed detail" constitutes a larger part of the present volume. The title piece, for example, is all about such intimate minuteness, the rendering consciousness of a moment in one's life, however stained by half-forgotten desires, re-readings and the more indulgent judgment of a later age. Borges, in one of his essays, speaks of "the bashfulness of history" that keeps to itself many of its turning-points. Much in the same way, a writer's true professional biography (the account of his work in progress) remains in the shadows, and only from time to time an instance is revealed that shows to the reader how that life, through a combination of chance, keen attention and the wit to make ends meet, results in a piece of prose or poetry. A writer's life is, in itself, of no interest, or at least of no more interest than that of any other human being, except as another viewpoint for his work, the suggestion of previous, unformed versions, the prehistory of his writing. It is always dangerous to assume that the connections are placidly clear. "I began a book with the letter 'I,'" wrote Proust, "and for the rest of my work I've been condemned to being that 'I.'" No reader should condemn the writers he loves to such life servitude.

But for Coles, certain events and certain memories serve not only as clues to the writing to come: they are in themselves things worthy of consideration. "There are artists whose diaries reward us with their complex reflections on the nature of the creative act, or with day-by-day notes on specific wrestling with specific works-in-progress, and such diaries often take their place alongside the novels and poems... as additional (different but not much less valuable) revelatory offerings from the same deep source." This sentence is from Coles review of Thomas Mann's *Diaries* (which he decides do not belong in this category.) Replace diaries for miscellany, and I believe *A Dropped*

Glove in Regent Street fits the description.

Coles' poetry concentrates, his novel expands; perhaps the meditative pieces in *A Dropped Glove in Regent Street* choose the middle ground, life-size observations of a certain moment and a certain place, most often through the personality of a certain writer whose life and work have interested him. The fact that most of these are, no doubt, command performances requested by a book-page editor, doesn't render them less lively or in any way dated. Coles' "casual talk" reinvents its own present: in whatever time and place we are, he is talking to us now.

The list of authors reviewed constitutes an eclectic library: Canetti, Graham Greene, Borges, Thomas Mann, Tolstoi, Thornton Wilder, Northrop Frye, D. M. Thomas, Ruskin, Victor Hugo, Brecht, e.e. cummings, Frost, Flaubert, Céline, Robert Graves, Camus, Proust... We might ask what Thomas, Ruskin or Greene have to do on Coles' shelf, but a writer's bread-and-butter work sometimes forces him into the kitchen with chefs whom he may otherwise not have chosen. In most cases, however, the association is clear. Tolstoi, Mann, and above all, Camus are among Coles' tutelary figures. "A man's work is nothing but the long road taken to find through the byways of art the two or three great, simple images to which the heart opened itself for the first time." Camus' casual talk (from the introduction to *L'Envers et l'endroit*) is echoed in Coles' words.

Fifteen years separate *A Dropped Glove in Regent Street* from *Little Bird*, but the conviction that we must try to make sense out of the world through words hasn't changed. *Little Bird* ends with this consolation:

> ... You
> can remind yourself
> they're only words. They
> know they're not true.

Words themselves may doubt of their veracity. The reader knows otherwise.

Serendipities

A Sleep as White as Snow

THE WORD SERENDIPITY gets overused, I think, but something close to it has just happened in my workroom, this room where I do my writing.

The assignment was to contribute some thoughts, a meditation, on winter in the North, winter either here in Canada or perhaps in Sweden, where I lived for half of my third decade (i.e., long ago); and no sooner did I begin to think about this than the serendipitous thing signalled itself.

My North Toronto window looks out, I should tell you, onto a ravine schoolyard, and that yard's covered with snow but it's blotchy with gray or bare patches and a few late kids arriving, and that's not what I wanted. I wanted a great field of whiteness and silence with a little wind stirring the top of that field so that here and there small gusts of flakes would rise privately and a little mysteriously up into the air and then dwindle down again.

So, think elsewhere, I told myself. And where do my thoughts typically go when I send them off to look for a scene like the one I've just described? Well, not always to the same place, of course, but quite often it's Stockholm, it's very late at night, in fact it's about 3 o'clock of a silent, snowy winter morning, and I've just stepped off the padded back of a Vespa on which a friend of mine, a Swedish *arkitekt*, has given me a lift home from a long party in Bromma, a Stockholm suburb, a party that was good for most of its length and not so good near its end and finally I was glad to go and here I am, almost home.

The "almost" is why I'm remembering it now. "Home" that winter was a cold-water flat four stories up in what's called Gamla Stan, "the Old Town", and from the place where I stepped off the Vespa I had to make my way up a steepish cobbled area just below Stockholm's Royal Castle to get into the narrow street where my flat was. Except that you couldn't see or feel the cobbles at that very early hour because they were under about four feet, three feet for sure, of snow.

The snow was as deep as anything I've ever tried to walk in, and it was still falling, big soft quiet flakes. And after the Vespa left, nobody at all was around, just the huge silence. The castle was barely visible up there through the falling snow, and, after a minute or two of getting practically nowhere, I was up to my hips in this soft trackless whiteness.

I suddenly felt very tired. There'd been gallons of wine at the party, I was probably a little drunk. I had been with a girl (we wouldn't call her that nowadays, but this was then) who worked as a librarian at the Alliance Française on Strandvägen, a girl I had met earlier that same day, and I had been, why not say so, probably a little thrilled to learn that she was named Nelly Valéry and was the grandniece of Paul Valéry, France's greatest poet of the twentieth century and somebody of whose poems I had actually read a few.

Nelly was, being both French and a Valéry, very acute. She was not tall, not blonde, in short she was a change from most of the people I'd met that year in Stockholm. She was quite pretty, though, so *plus ça change* is a phrase that seems worth mentioning here.

What hadn't been so good about the party, in spite of its generous and never-encountered host, had been a little scene that I had witnessed in a bedroom where Nelly and I and some French guy, who seemed to have known her longer than I had and was annoying me a little by hanging about, were standing talking, and in a silence we had all noticed that two young men sitting in conversation together on the bed were speaking not French, not Swedish, but German.

And the next thing everybody noticed was that this guy, the annoying one, was shouting at these two young Germans and saying they should bloody shut up, didn't they know any better, didn't they know that their goddamned language shouldn't be spoken here, or, indeed, anywhere else, and so on like that, standing very close to them and shouting. Screaming, really. And they were looking up at him and they were saying nothing.

You should remember that this was in the 1950s. France had recently been an occupied country, etc. Many related etcs. And who knows what private histories could have been involved, on the screaming guy's part I mean. Maybe nothing, maybe something. In any case, nobody was certain about that and nobody did anything.

So two people who couldn't have been older, that night, than 20 or so, and therefore had had no more to do with anything relating to the Second World War and its accompanying awfulnesses than I had, got screamed at.

I've no idea how that scene ended, except that it ended, people drifted off. I must have drifted off, too, obviously Nelly and I didn't leave together, otherwise I wouldn't have found myself at 3 in the morning getting off a Vespa and facing that white snowfield all on my own. I've never forgotten the scene, though, or the looks on those two boys' faces, or the sense I had of a congested and unclarified and everyway unhappy drama.

Where the whole thing might have become quite a lot more personally meaningful is back there in that cobbled area below the castle, where I left myself several paragraphs ago. I was so exhausted, especially after making it about a third of the way up toward my street, and the snowflakes were so big and white and falling with such surreal noiselessness, that I got an idea that right away became enormously persuasive. My idea was that I would sit down.

I pictured it so easily, it was clear that when I sat down I'd be very private, the snow was so high nobody'd be able to see me, and I could sleep away the whole rest of the night, and how comfortable it would be, and I wouldn't have to go on trying to climb in snow that was half as high as I was myself. I can truthfully say that it was very, very close to happening.

Of course it didn't happen, or, what a loss, you'd not be reading this column. I didn't sit down, I made it home, I stayed under my big yellow blanket for quite a while, life resumed.

I almost forgot the serendipity. Thinking about that night, and Nelly, I went downstairs just minutes ago to get Nelly's granduncle's *Poésies*. And you don't need to believe this but it's true, the second or third page I looked at has a poem called 'Neige'. It's about how the snow has been falling silently all night and has been waiting for the narrator to wake up. A not-bad touch already, I thought, Nelly's granduncle's got a good one here; and then reading on I found him saying, casually, brilliantly, that he fears the snow's innocence.

In an odd way I felt that some connection was being made right then, not an exact fit with my little far-off night, but close.

A Dropped Glove in Regent Street

THIS IS THE SAD STORY of myself grown old, a condition I did not strive after. Keats, Rimbaud, Plath (only one of whom I actually met) all demonstrate the value of an early departure—who wants to be the crazy old Ruskin or the rambling octogenarian Wordsworth or even the merely shaky May Sarton? And yet here I am, threescore-and-ten-plus, nobody can call me anything other than old and people have stopped trying.

Best, then, is to do as I do, don neutral-coloured clothing and stand at the fringes of whatever comes your way; no one is likely to ask your opinion or thrust a microphone at you anyway, they have more attractive options…and who blames them?

What makes me smile, nevertheless, a mirthless smile it goes without saying, is remembering, even as I step unresentfully back whenever some younger person wishes to stand where I am standing, how there was a time when…yes, reader, here it comes. When I was young! When I, too, was visible on a sidewalk!

The pathos of this old fellow's unverifiable claim, you are now thinking, and again, I cannot blame you. Pathos indeed.

And yet I will tell you, for it's too late to turn back now, that one afternoon walking up the via Tornabuoni in Florence, aged 23 and wearing a dark raincoat on a grey day, I saw approaching me down the via Tornabuoni a gaggle of people of whom only one was truly present to my gaze, this being a tall and blonde and carelessly sumptuous in her attire woman of about 35, English I felt and feel sure, closely guarded in her walking by three diminutive middle-aged men, all credible stand-ins for Carlo Ponti.

I stared unashamedly at this wonder and had a fleeting impression that she briefly returned my look just as the four of them left the sidewalk along which they had been approaching me, crossed the road, and disappeared into Doney's Bar, a toney place halfway up the

Tornabuoni and one I had never entered.

I stopped to watch them enter Doney's Bar, feeling a formless lament, but feeling, also, not quite ready to start up walking again. So I loitered, I remember there was a florist's where I was standing and I occasionally looked at a plant or two while I stood there. I have never had any interest in plants. It was then that the first of my two shameful and unforgiven acts—non-acts, as you will see—took place.

Because as I stood beside the florist's window the blonde woman, unaccompanied now by any of the Carlo Ponti look-alikes, reappeared at Doney's door and gazed directly across the street at me.

At me? This couldn't be, I at once felt. I looked back at the florist's window, someone must surely be signalling to her from within, desperately waving a bouquet of violets. But no, nothing moved within, no one appeared, there was only one person on the street and it was I. The woman was still standing there, gazing across. The Tornabuoni held its breath.

It had held its breath thousands of times before but at the moment this didn't concern me. The woman said nothing, merely waited and looked. What was she supposed to do, wave? She had done her share, she had done all she could, I knew this. It was my turn, some signal, a quick run across the street, the exchange of a few words, a rendezvous, where, anywhere, down there by the Arno, in an hour, who cared, anything at all. I didn't budge.

I did and said nothing.

Why not, didn't I trust this? Here was the lustrous heroine of *The Sun Also Rises*, Lady Brett, her ancestral meadows spreading endlessly about her as obviously as the green curtains on Doney's windows, and I was a stone. She looked, she waited a few more seconds, she turned and re-entered the bar. Thinking whatever she was thinking. And I—? Walked on my way, towards whatever exotic appointment awaited me. Picking up a reserved book at the American library, probably.

It gets worse. Some months later, back in London after my student year in Florence, walking up Regent Street on a pre-Christmas day, a few snowflakes testing the air, passing Austin Reed's long storefront I noticed a small queue of people waiting at the bus stop. I wasn't intent on catching a bus so I paid no attention, I merely continued to approach them. As I was in the act of passing them, something fell to the sidewalk just before my step. I paused, it was a woman's glove.

I looked to see who had dropped it—the sky opened and fell upon me. It was Lady Brett. The blonde from the Via Tornbuoni. Beyond any doubt. Our eyes met. We were so close we could have embraced without moving anything but our arms. Across the road was the Café Royale, celebrated rendezvous of Waugh, Orwell, Connolly, heroes all: a place with small tables in tactfully positioned alcoves and the discreetest of waiters. You will not believe what happened next.

I did not pick up the glove. I paused, I didn't want to step on it, after all. For a second or two it waited there. Then she bent to pick it up. I walked grotesquely on. Seconds later the bus arrived, and the queue, certainly including her, got on it. It rolled up Regent Street past me.

At this point I was almost staggering. Drowning in self-contempt. I tried to assure myself that we must meet again, surely this would happen, after all we had now had two meetings in a half-year, it must be fated, I would perhaps see her tomorrow, perhaps at this same bus stop. And never again would I fail her.

I was at that same bus stop at the same hour the next day, needless to say she was not. Or any other day, or on any other London or Florence street. Not that I know. Ever.

What does this have to do with old age? Nothing.

Something to do with youth, though.

And Sunlight Thronged the Glass

MY TITLE IS A LINE from Philip Larkin. He's known more for gloom than *joie-de-vivre* and yet here's this image that throbs with all the busy vitality that 'sunlight' (plus a verb it's never been jammed-up this close to before) can give it.

I've been asked to write about this today: about *light*, and about what three people of my choice, two of them in our own time and one far-off, have had to say of it. And I'm starting with the one who, of my chosen, gifted, three, has showed me the most unforgettably light-thronged image I know. This image-maker was and is Ingmar Bergman, and he writes of this near-miraculous scene in his autobiography, *The Magic Lantern*. "A moment of grace", he says it was.

More to the point, he *shows* it in my all-time favourite movie, which I saw in Stockholm in its first screening. Its Swedish title is *Smultronstället*, translated as *Wild Strawberries*. There's an implication in the Swedish title which doesn't easily translate, the 'smultron' being a particular strawberry which indeed grows wild and is, besides being sweeter and brighter-red and smaller than the usual berry, hard to find, hence secret, hidden, special. So to a Swede the title may be a quiet password into a private and long-kept secret such as the scene I'm about to describe.

The movie shows the journey an ageing professor is making from Stockholm down to the university town of Lund where he'll be given an honorary degree. Skipping the detail,s there's a lot of sadness here, the professor's being driven to Lund by his daughter-in-law who's heading into a divorce from his son, and he realizes as they drive and talk that his own coldness towards his years-dead wife probably has crippled all four lives. En route, they stop at a place in the country where, as a teen-ager, the professor had spent a summer with family and friends, a summer during which he fell in love with a girl whom he should, he has long known, have asked to marry him, and did not.

The light-thronged scene is one which he's now, in memory, seeing, and we see it with him. It shows his youthful self together with eight or nine other young people, all of them dressed in white and all standing or sitting or lying on the bank of a river among small sounds of water and of young, uncomplicated, barely audible voices. The scene has more *light* in it, or the light more softness, possibly more forgiveness, than anything I know of in cinema, it always strikes me as astonishingly comforting, it brings tears to my eyes every time I watch it, and my belief is that Bergman found, in that place and on that day of filming, a perfect *temps perdu* image.

My second contribution is from Annie Dillard. There's an essay in *Teaching A Stone to Talk* which records a day in which the essayist and her husband climbed a hill in the state of Washington in order to watch a total eclipse of the sun. It's not really about light, but it belongs here because it's so bluntly and brilliantly about the *absence* of light, the violent vanishing of light, and therefore *is*, after all, about light.

Standing on the hillside in the morning with her husband, Dillard watches the darkness slide "like a lid" over the sun. It frightens them: "The heart screeched". She equates her experience here with a journey towards "the monsters deeper down", and adds, "I pray you will never see anything more awful in the sky." She continues: "The second before the sun went out we saw a wall of dark shadow come speeding at us. We no sooner saw it than it was upon us, like thunder…Language can give no sense of this kind of speed. It rolled at you across the land at 1,800 miles an hour, hauling darkness like plague behind it…We saw the wall of shadow coming, and screamed before it hit."

That's it, that's why these fragments of her essay are here. Light's absence, in a way our forbears knew every nightfall of their lives, and we hardly ever do. It shows in an extreme manner how we, I would guess most of us, deep down, beneath the frail carapace of reason and control which Freud rightly mocked, feel about the light and the dark. There exist books, some of them still in print after hundreds of years, with titles like *At Day's Close: A History of Nighttime*, like *Terrors of the Night*, like *Dread of Supernatural Powers*, which remind us that in earlier times darkness was far more pervasive, much more *the* primary element, especially in the north, than it is now. In those times and places, travel, whether local or abroad, was perilous: towns locked their gates at nightfall and strung chains across darkening streets. In the houses of the poor, flickeringly lit by a candle or two, by brief and unreliable rushlights if you couldn't afford candles, it's understandable how much more readily—more easily than today, than tonight—ghosts were near and faces could come out of the dark for a few seconds, for a half-sentence, to whisper their secrets. Towards the end of her essay, when the dark goes and the sun returns, Dillard writes, "We joined our places on the planet's thin crust. It held. For the time being...."

I told you I'd promised a "far-off" entry, and here, pat on his cue (the cue being Dillard's "monsters deeper down'), he comes, Beowulf, who else, disembarking among the glittering shields and helms of his Geat warriors onto a land over which a half-human monster, who emerges at nightfall from the depths of a black pond in a black forest as regularly as, well, blackness recurs, has established death and dismemberment as the imprint of the true darkness—the darkness which this creature, Grendel, in fact *is,* as Beowulf is the sun. The parallel is exact throughout this ancient and splendid poem (now newly and stunningly translated by Seamus Heaney, with the Anglo-Saxon on a facing page and those *Ur*-syllables often greatly closer in look and sound to modern-day English than anyone else has ever shown them to be). Unlike the Dillard piece this is a sun-and-light-triumph from beginning to end, from the hero's slaughter of both Grendel and his night-hag Dam to his own death in the last reel, when we see his knights riding in all their gold-caparisoned pomp around Beowulf's funeral pyre, which sends its flames to the heavens. The poem glitters like those riders, it practically singes my hands as it burns through my book's front-and-back covers, and, in the dark monkish culture from which it spectacularly came, it must have seemed a torch.

P.S. So light triumphs, yes. But to the old and the ill, things are not as we have said. Darkness and night are more familiar to them than they are to us, their hearts do not screech as the humiliations of the day are discarded and they enter that sought-after, unwatched, unjudged privacy. Not much that matters to them is going on right now anyway, few races that interest them are being run. They enter into the dark where their young, confident thoughts rise to greet them.

Scenes from a Cambridge Life

[Scene One]

THIS ONE LIGHTS UP on my first Cambridge sherry party, a late afternoon affair in King's College's SCR, to which I, a Queen's man, had been invited by an ex-Toronto friend. Minutes after my arrival, standing with a glass of quite good (this was King's, after all) sherry and with no known face nearby, I began hearing two braying ex-Public School voices close behind me. They were involved in a sort of *faux*-debate, and *noblesse* obliged, both seemed to feel, that not only those voices but also each florid sentence and fluttering syllable reach more of an audience than just each other. The debate centred upon, it soon became clear, which of the two speakers had been the first to sleep with the glamorous World War One poet Rupert Brooke. A touch startling, I found this: it was, you must remember, my first week in rez, and back in Canada my mother owned cherished first editions of Brooke's two 1916 bestselling collections. I have them still, though over the years the world's respect for them has wavered. Back at that sherry-party, though, I remember deciding that as far as my mother was concerned, I would keep the news of this King's College one-up-man-ship to myself. When my host showed up I asked him who these two gents (one of them a beaky, silvery-haired ancient, the other glossily-bald, a bit younger and considerably stouter) were. The beaky one was Sir John Sheppard, the then-Provost (president) of King's; the baldy was George 'Dadie' Rylands, English Lit tutor at King's, founder of the nowadays-still-functioning Marlowe Society and formerly a fringe member of the Bloomsbury group (as a very young man he set type and ran errands for Virginia and Leonard Woolf at the Hogarth Press).

He was a not-bad lecturer, was Rylands, I later discovered, if you could put up with his tales of his all-sorts lovers and his platform-preening. As an intellect and teacher he wasn't in the same league as the two men I'd studied with for four years back at the U.of Toronto, Northrop Frye and Marshall McLuhan, but then who, anywhere, was? For now, though, this confidential sherry-sharing with two such *genii loci* seemed promising.

Nice start there, squire, I said to myself. First week here and already really in the swim.

27

[Scene Two]

A bunch of undergraduates, all of them male, were in the habit of meeting every Tuesday night in the principal room of The Anchor, one of the two riverside pubs closest to Queen's. They met primarily to sing folksongs, and as a rule everyone who wasn't Irish was Welsh, with three exceptions. One of these exceptions, and much the most important that night, was a Scot named Mac Emslie, who was doing grad work in Eng.Lit. and generally accompanied the singers on the pub piano. The two others, both of them outsiders who joined in only on the choruses, and then only after earnest listening, were the Yorkshireman Ted Hughes and the colonial you are just now reading.

On the night in question the singing was led by Danny Huws, who a few decades later would be Keeper of the Manuscripts and Records of the National Library of Wales. They were particularly hearty, the voices that night, and Mac, the pianist, was far too busy hammering away to keep up with the pints that were accumulating on his piano-top. I suppose I must have been standing closer to the piano than anyone else most of the time, in any case Mac kept on, feverishly as I recall, pushing his unsipped pints in my direction as the night wore on, and I kept on feverishly keeping up, downing his pints as well as my own. Both Mac and I had 'gone down', i.e. graduated, the year before and needed to catch the last train back to London that night, so at evening's-end we left in a hurry, found an empty compartment and slumped on the upholstered benches facing each other as the train clanked southwards. Here is what I remember of that journey. I remember Mac, who had had barely a drop to drink all night, giving me in what I think was a lot of detail a chapter-by-chapter explication of the English Lit thesis he was working on at the University of London; and I remember not a single sentence of that explication, only the dismaying oscillation of the railway car and my locked-in stare at Mac as I attempted to prevent myself from falling flat on the carpet between our benches. I think I felt that if I could keep that dogged stare intact I'd fool Mac into thinking I was following his lecture, and at the same time foil the gravitational forces that were urging me floorwards.

I may have been succesful in both regards. I know that I managed the entire journey to King's Cross without ever saying a word other than a 'sure' or a 'really' or a yes/no now and then to simulate the rhythm of a dialogue , and, my only other ambition, without damaging the carpet in any too crass a manner. I also know that four or five months later, in Paris, I was having a meal at our favourite Montparnasse bistro, called *À la Soupe Merveilleuse,* with my best Queen's pal, an Irishman named Fintan O'Connell—actually it was a birthday party for one of the two brothers who owned the bistro, both of them as bravely moustached as though they were on leave from that Renoir boating party—when Finn told me he had recently run into Mac Emslie in London and Mac had told him that the train journey he and I had shared following that Tuesday night in The Anchor had provided him with 'the all-time best conversation that he, Mac, had ever taken part in'.

So there 'tis. Everyone's idea of the perfect chat.

[Scene Three]

A few words about another gathering only a couple of streets from that pub and then I'm on to my last Cantab scene. The occasion was the launch party for a poetry journal called *The St.Botolph's Review,* too celebrated in poetry circles now for me to need to spend time on it. Most of the Queen's people I knew best, Joe Lyde, Mike Boddy, Sam Lewis, Finn O'Connell, were probably there from the start, I arrived a fair bit later, not in perfect shape and needing to sit down at once, which I did, in a generously-upholstered chair. A friend from Newnham, I think we were the only two non-poets in the room, came in and sat on the arm of the chair, and at one point a lanky American girl came by and paused beside us. I knew she was American because she said something, I don't think it was a question but something. History tapped its fingers for a few seconds and then it and the lanky American girl moved on. The next day I had a very lengthy and, as I remember it, good talk—close to impassioned, I'd say, but eased along with lots of smiling, quick nods, pleasures of that high sort which people at that stage of life more often have than they will later—with Luke Myers in The Mill (the other of the two Queen's riverside pubs). Luke, as I knew him, or Lucas, as I find him being called in the bios, was Ted Hughes's closest friend that year, a very likeable Virginian. I was sorry we had to break off that talk when we did, so that I could catch, again, the train back to London that same afternoon. Ted's onrushing life with the lanky American girl was, that afternoon, still one of those things that might happen, might not.

[Last scene]

The above-mentioned Fintan O'Connell, the decentest, honestest, sweetest guy I met during my two years in Cambridge (interesting, I think, or maybe not, how the most celebrated people one has met in one's life are seldom among the half-million most likeable people one has met), invited me, my last year there, to his home in Newcastle for the Easter vac. This particular Newcastle was a little village just a few miles west of Belfast, not the metropolis of the same name in Yorkshire. Now and then during that fortnight several other Queensmen and Irishmen showed up at Finn's place, viz. Joe Lyde, trumpeter and drinker *extraordinaire,* and a few more, Mick somebody and possibly the already-mentioned Michael Boddy (a very large lad, gifted writer too, who edited a broadsheet called *Broadsheet* which ran all the way to one number and which I made the pages of during our last Queen's year); but most memorable of all those present during my stay in that village and that house was Finn's much-older brother, who owned a string of pubs in both northern Ireland and Eire, and who was all that Finn had by way of relatives in that uniquely odd world that I think Ireland must very often be. This brother, whose name I've lost track of, was about 45 years old, was stone deaf, a bachelor, and had three passions that I got to know of during my time in that house. These passions were: a friendship with a local private eye who was chiefly engaged in divorce work (Finn had a wonderful account, frequently rendered, of the private eye and the deaf brother shouting at each other from their horizontal hideyholes under the misbehaving adulterers' bed—"What's 'ee say? What's 'ee sayin' there?", or, "What's 'ee doin' anyhow?"), who had also a passion for Gladstone bags, which he bought in large lots at estate auctions and had hundreds of in several of the many unused bedrooms of the brothers' house (I mistakenly, one day, opened the door of one of those rooms and the bags came tumbling out, a couple of dozen of them onto the frayed carpet in the hallway; I stuffed them back in as best I could); and this brother also had space in his house for two monster-size St. Bernards. When Finn and I would leave the house at noon each day for our regular Guinesses at the village's one pub, me riding on the back of Finn's Lambretta and the two dogs following us, their ropes of white saliva swinging broadly from one shoulder of the village's gravel road to the other, we would sometimes find access to the pub's bar denied us by the regulars standing in a proprietary line from one bar-end to the other. Into the bar, however, on those occasions, summoned by their master's cry, would then trot the St. Bernards, still swinging their ten-foot swathes of saliva from one side of the room to t'other, and bedamned if the bar didn't clear in a flash.

There exist other tales of this odd brother of Newcastle, they speak among other things of his collection of outsize sepia Victorian paintings with titles like *The Monarch of the Glen* and featuring elk posing in suicidal profile on hillocks in one or other of those glens, paintings of which at least one *must* hang, by contractual agreement between pub-licencee and pub-owner, directly behind the bar of each of those many pubs—this in spite, Finn told me, of the frequently and understandably violent objections of the licencees. Finn and I were supposed, although I know we shirked the assignment, to report back on any pub which was not doing its duty in this regard. And there are other tales, too, which if I chose I daresay I could still retrieve and add to this account, since my friend Finn is still alive and functioning as the right-hand man of an industrialist in Milan, a city he detests but continues to inhabit for the sake of the three persons he cherishes the most in the world: his beloved South African/Italian *moglie,* his equally *carina figlia* , and, not too far away in the city of Trieste, James Joyce, or at least the house in which that third member of Finn's charmed trinity lived when he first left Dublin. But I'd best do it soon, for it's many years since Finn and I left our undergraduate years behind, so the much older brother and his gumshoe companion must long since be horizontal and whispery in Newcastle's cemetery, and Joe Lyde's trumpet I know is forever quiet too, drowned in whiskey along with its master even more prematurely than one might have guessed, and there are a few others who for a while wrote to me from various addresses in England or Ireland mentioning the possibility of showing up in Sweden, where I was, or in Italy, where I was, but never doing that; and all these are either gone or at the very least are very far hence. And you may make sure of these matters by browsing in any one of the several published biographies of the ex-poet laureate known, more or less, to Finn and Joe and Mick and Michael though I will guess not better known to them than they, long ago, singing the songs of their country, were to him.

Reviews Redux*

*Most of these reviews, except for an identified few, originally appeared in *The Globe and Mail*, and all have been expanded.

Canetti

The Play Of The Eyes by Elias Canetti

The Play of the Eyes, the third instalment of Elias Canetti's memoirs, makes a stunning read. Especially if you have a passion for the Vienna of *entre-deux-guerres*, the city of Robert Musil, Karl Kraus, Oscar Kokoschka, Stefan Zweig, Alban Berg, and a bunch more.

They are all here and Canetti knows all of them. He adores Kraus and models his early writings on that icily exacting satirist. He falls in love with Alma Mahler-Werfel's daughter Anna (Alma got her double surname from Gustave Mahler and Franz Werfel, two of her three husbands, the deleted one being Walter Gropius; she was also involved with Kokoschka, and, much later, when she had an apartment in New York, was a friend of Ted Heinrich, one-time ROM director who later taught in Humanities at York University). And he meets the working-class sculptor Fritz Wortruba. That last-mentioned friendship forced Canetti's relationship with language to alter in the direction of Wortruba's "daily blows on hardest stone". If you care for Vienna, or for writing, or just generally if you appreciate living for more than 300 pages with some of the most extravagantly gifted spirits of a time and place that the barbarians were soon to kick to death, then this is an exhilarating read.

It is nothing less than striking to notice, granted the crystal-clear fact that *The Play of the Eyes* is permeated by intelligence of an unmistakably high order, that not a single member of the group Canetti presents to us seems ever to have found it necessary to parade the fact of her or his intellectual preeminence. There are a high proportion of journalists among them, Kraus at the forefront, but there's not a prater or prancer in sight, a nice contrast to what can be seen in today's blatts on a regular basis. Canetti knows he's privileged as he wanders the streets of his city, moving from one exalted encounter to the next: from an hour with his near-anonymous guru 'Dr.Sonne' at the latter's reliable café-table where the day's clichés have been wryly dismantled over the *kaffee mit schlag,* to a tense rendezvous with Anna in her studio, to his own desk and his struggles with story, essay, play or novel. To be one with Sonne and Wortruba and Broch and Berg and now and then even the great Karl Kraus, was a magical island in time which Canetti recognized as such and exulted in. Once in a while we even find him sympathizing with a Werfel or a Zweig, successful and admired as they are, because among all these *luminati* they're understood to be not quite first-rate. This heady joy is communicated on every page, so that the reader is not merely shaking his head at the thought of Canetti's great luck in picking not just one but two decades like this for his young life, but is sharing in the joy.

Well, sharing it insofar as he or she can. Other than vicariously like this hardly anybody has ever lived among as intelligence-irradiated a group as these people were, and it's permissible in any of us, I suppose, to wish that we had had the same luck. Writing of Dr. Sonne (whom Canetti had at first known as merely a client of the same café, a man who sat hidden behind his newspaper in perfect self-contain-ment day after day), Canetti explains his boundless gratitude for the privilege of "associating with someone who has the gift of exploring a subject, of not dropping it before the whole ground has been covered and not analyzing it to pieces. Sonne never reduced a subject, never *disposed* of it. His talking…articulated and illuminated it. He founded whole countries in the mind of his listener. He had no use for anything that could turn conversation into gossip… and his conception of individuals was that each is a distinct field of knowledge. The sterile notion that any single theory might be applicable to all people was utterly alien to him. Even when he had to name the things he hated, there was no hatred in his tone; he was merely laying bare an absurdity."

There is much more at this level, a level of wisdom from which we ought all (if wisdom like that were only spread about fairly) to be hearing regularly. There are also infusions of sheer energy, and as I've said, it's the energy of a special mind recalling its fabulous years. A special mind with an utter absence of *amour-propre*—amazing! Or perhaps not amazing. Perhaps the author of *Auto-da-Fé,* the Büchner-and-Nobel-Prize winning dramatist and novelist, author also of sociological masterworks such as *Crowds and Power*, for such a one perhaps vanity truly becomes what he calls it, "an absurdity". Canetti falls in love with Anna Mahler-Werfel, who shortly thereafter tells him in the most dispassionate of letters that he has ceased to interest her. He may, she adds, continue to write to her, since she has always preferred his words to his physical presence, but nothing further. This devastates him. Well, yes, it would, wouldn't it. What's unusual is that Canetti tells us this, offers no excuses or explanations, openly acknowledges that there were no compensations and nothing was ever made good or redeemed. You feel he sees no point in decorating the story or lying about it, and he pays us the compliment of not explaining *that*, either. Anna recedes into history, mysterious, undiminished. What we're left with is an experience of a subtlety and a candour we seldom get even a breath of.

It's not all about famous folk, there are glimpses of the only-a-little-famous, too. Of , e.g., a womanizing conductor who pursued only married women because "women who don't have to be taken from anyone depressed his libido". Of Musil's *The Man Without Qualities*: "The true, the essential eternity of such a work…is passed on to the reader, who can content himself with no stopping place and reads again and again what would otherwise come to an end". And again and again, of Sonne, who "if fame matters" deserved fame but was happier without it. "Through Sonne I learned for the first time what a man's integrity means; it means he will not be swayed by questions, even by problems, that he will go his own way without revealing his motives or past history. Even to myself I did not put questions about his person; even in my thoughts he remained inviolable."

I've praised Canetti in almost every paragraph thus far but there's one thing I hold against him. 'Tis quickly said. In a biography of one of my favourite, indeed most loved and learned-from, near-contemporary novelists, Iris Murdoch (I *know* she lost it in the last five or six books, not her fault though; she was falling towards Alzheimers and her editors, damn them comprehensively, ought to have served her better, ought not to have let those last MSS see daylight), I've learned that Canetti, a serial seducer—this is not what I hold against him—whom Murdoch passionately and openly loved, spoke derisively of her *qua* lover ('ignorant and boring'), mocked even her personal habits and hygiene, in general abused one who at that sad stage of her life couldn't speak or write back. So: as a man, in this case if not in others, Canetti's nauseating, a kind of landmark in contemptibility. (It reminds me of a passage quoted elsewhere in this book but so little acknowledged in our timorous age that it's worth repeating here. It's from George Orwell, the master of the no-crap-here's-what-I-think-of-you remark; and it's the sort of remark from which most literary types recoil because they know they will, if they utter it, especially if they utter it in print, be forever on their victim's kill-list, they'll be debarred from any grant-in-aid or G-G or Giller or, Heaven forfend, Booker prize if that victim one day happens to be on a jury judging such matters or, almost as fate-ordaining, happens to be reviewing their own still-unwritten masterpiece. Here's the passage, not aimed at Canetti but at another deserving target: "One ought to be able to hold in one's head simultaneously the two facts that Dali is a good draughtsman and a disgusting human being.")

As a writer, though—

—if you are a writer, read this book for what it will tell you of a relationship to language as pure as Rainer Maria Rilke's; more forceful than Rilke's and moving over a more identifiably human, angel-deserted terrain, but just as intense, just as pure. If you are a reader, read it for that same reason.

Greene

A World of My Own: A Dream Diary by Graham Greene

When he was at work on a novel Graham Greene had the habit of re-reading the day's output just before going to bed, believing that this would allow his subconscious to engage itself profitably during sleep. Thomas Mann, I happen to know, felt the same way: during the writing of the monumental *Joseph and His Brethren* Mann's bedtime readings were inexorably Biblical. He was in no doubt that these returned relevant images to him ten-fold. Mustard seeds every one.

I find all this interesting and probably valuable: it is, however, the only respect in which this "dream diary" puts one in mind of anybody or anything remotely as solemn or half as stupendous as *der Zauberer* and his works. What it offers, instead, is something quite slight and really of no instructive worth whatsoever, but which turns out to be as likeable a read as you may have had in years. It's funny and moving and always marvellously subtle in its intelligence, the work of a craftsman who knows his craft so intimately that nothing he touches escapes it. It might seem a ponderous intrusion to now mention Theodor Adorno and his (to me, riveting) theories of *Spät-stil* (Late Style)—he'd noticed, Adorno wrote, how writers and artists of all kinds often, in their late years, achieve a sort of ease which resembles carelessness, resembles a deliberate breaking-of-rules, as if there was nothing left to prove and so one was free to, e.g. write 'badly', but badly from that beyond-confidence place one had reached, and so, in fact, write repetitively, if that's how the words came, or brusquely, or awkwardly, or superlatively fluently if *that* was what arrived on the page....well, I said it might seem ponderous, I'll now leave it half-finished and unproven, perhaps that's my own version of *Spät-stil.* At any rate reading Graham Greene at this late, light-floating stage of his career, I was very soon turning each page in a state of happy anticipation, and what thin volume of *any* provenance have you had in your hands this year that allowed that?

A World of My Own is just what its sub-title says it is: a record of Greene's dreams as these appeared in diaries kept between 1965 and 1989. The diaries run to 800 pages; how many of these pages included dreams Greene doesn't say, but my guess is he was ruthless in his weedings-out—this large-print book is brevity itself. It's also quotability itself, which is what I propose to do with the wordage I have left.

Just one point first. Much of the persuasiveness of these dreams centres in their utter disregard for the reasoned structure and the logical development of the conscious, daylight creation—that, plus the *sine qua non* ingredient of any dream, which I take to be its bottom-line weirdness. Add now to this the little glints that keep reminding you of the distinctive nature of this particular dreamer, the highly imaginative, widely traveled, radically nonconformist novelist, and you have what I think many readers will find here, a modest unmistakable jewel.

To begin with a one-dream section identified as *Happiness*. The narrator arrives in an English town called Hordern where nothing at all happens except that he meets a young couple and all three go off to a pub together. In the pub he feels "inexplicable happiness"—more, Greene tells us (stepping for a sentence or two outside the dream) than he has ever felt in "the Common World". The very absence of exotic detail makes this three-page story as moving and swiftly trustable as anything in the book.

In *Some Famous Writers I Have Known* he meets Henry James on a boat in South America. Everything's ominous and crowded and he urges Henry James to join him in an escape, but James won't hear of it, they must go on to the bitter end. "For scientific reasons", James tells him.

That's my favourite line in the book. This may tell you whether the rest of this review will be worth your while.

In the same section the dreamer meets Ford Madox Ford. He keeps wanting to tell Ford of his admiration for a book of Ford's about the Spanish Civil War, but the title keeps eluding him. "Several times I had begun to say *For Whom the Bell*... but checked myself."

Talking to Auden at a party he explains why he prefers living in

England to living in America. It is because English literature is far richer than American literature: "Shakespeare made all other writers into dwarfs and there can be no jealousy among dwarfs. American literature, having no such giant, gives room for jealousy."

In a section called *In the Secret Service* he meets Goebbels and tries to assassinate him with the fumes from a "special cigarette" he's smoking. Later in this dream he arouses a woman's suspicions by replying, when asked where he was going, "Shopping".

That is not my favourite line in the book, I've already told you what that is, but it is my favourite word.

Walking with Fidel Castro he meets a man crying at the grave of his child. Castro fails to comfort the man, but when the man sees the dreamer cross himself he "stopped crying and shook my hand. He said 'I feel you are one of those who thinks there may be something after death.'"

Later on, in a room in which a troublesome parrot has been flying about, "someone thrust a large spider into my trousers and I felt it grasp my penis. This was worse even than the parrot."

As an arachnophobe of an advanced sort I am sorry I read that far, but almost all of the other dreams I'm now quite fond of. There's a genuinely moving piece of dream-composed verse on the book's last page about his own death, as simple and elegiac as some marvelous lines of Nabokov's on the same theme. Here, concluding both book and review, is Graham Greene.

From the room next door
The TV talks to me
Of sickness, nettle-rash,
And herbal tea.
My breath is folded up
Like sheets of lavender.
The end for me
Arrives like nursery tea.

Mann

Thomas Mann Diaries 1918-1939

THERE ARE ARTISTS whose diaries reward us with their complex reflections on the nature of the creative act, or with day-by-day notes on specific wrestlings with specific works-in-progress, and such diaries often take their place alongside the novels and poems and paintings as additional (different but not much less valuable) revelatory offerings from the same deep source. Virginia Woolf has been for quite a while and still is an obvious case in point. Another is the Norwegian painter and *déprimé* Edvard Munch. A third would be André Gide.

That Thomas Mann is *not* such a one explains the disappointment evidently felt by many readers of these present diaries, which have been appearing in Germany over the past twenty years; the disappointment, however, is not only (I think) unjustified, it's surely also suggestive of much blindness to the nature of the particular beast. A writer who is as nearly-misshapenly committed to writing, as opposed to living, as Thomas Mann was, is not going to have *those* sort of energies left at the end of the day. What will be left, instead, after Aschenbach and Castorp and Leverkühn have pillaged the day of everything in sight is going to be, surely, just what any other right-thinking *Staatsbürger* has got left at bedtime. Or not much more than that. And so it is here. Disappointing only if you have not immersed yourself in Mann's *real* words; but if you *have* read those words, then, if you ask me, the diaries are just as gripping and satisfying as anything must be which has been so long and so jealously kept away from all unsupervised eavesdropping.

So: what's so gripping about a diary devoid of all those agonized selfsearchings of the grander spirit? Lots of things. Thomas's relationships with his wife, Katia, and his brother, Heinrich, for two of those things. He bullies Katia because—well, is it because she's been snooping into his files, *á la* Countess Tolstoy with *her* husband, and like many another spouse with many another (talented or, just as many, giftless) artist too? No, it's because she's used too much butter the last little while. Almost at once he feels remorseful about this so he insists on a talk, during which, when their talk has reminded them that it is now 33 years since their marriage, he confides to her that he "wouldn't like to repeat this life in which painfulness has predominated". The same evening he writes in this diary, "Afraid I hurt Katia by saying this." Well, um, yes, Thomas, you probably did. Another day he records his gratitude to her for her "loving sympathy" when he is in one of his many periods of impotence. And yet another time he notes that he is laying aside forever a poem because "Katia thinks the line 'Shoulders of flute-playing women, Nile valley shoulders' impermissible". There I'm on his side. But this is all exhilarating stuff. It's also more intimately trust-invoking than the sanitized musings of the don't-fail-to-publish-this-when-I'm gone genre of diary that one is all too familiar with.

And Heinrich. The sheer awfulness of the way these two *Brüdern* carried on with each other is well known. Apollonian Thomas, Dionysian Heinrich: cold, classical, elitist Thomas, a jingoist patriot in World War One; warm, romantic, populist Heinrich, a pacifist/socialist spokesman for any protest movement that came along. The diaries extend one's knowledge of this disaster area. When a critic attacks one of Heinrich's plays, Thomas notes in his diary, "Steinruck's comment that H. is no dramatist is true", and then, unappeased, adds, "But he is also no novelist". Who needs a Steinruck when a brother is nearby?

The dates of this diary are misleading. For the years 1921 to 1933 there is no record, Thomas burned those notebooks. Too bad, because it's those years that might have been the most vital: in 1921 Thomas is writing *Der Zauberberg* (The Magic Mountain), arguably (*certainly*, if you ask me) his finest book in any genre. He has also, at this stage, not yet perfected his habit of cutting short any potentially revealing passage in mid-indiscretion. This latter may have something to do with the above-noted fiery end of some of the diaries: re-reading them one winter's day up there in the couple's last home in Küsnacht, overlooking the Zürichsee, he must have felt he had gone too far. We can't be sure what direction the 'too far' took, but guesses have been made. Unlike Gustave Aschenbach, *Death in Venice*'s ageing writer trailing after the beautiful boy Tadzio among the winding streets and the little bridges over the city's canals, Thomas could still call a halt.

This is not 'mere' innuendo: a dozen or more passages make it clear that young men or boys of Tadzio's extreme beauty moved Thomas compellingly. I've come to think that this explains, at least in part, the shadowy and inconclusive nature of some of the *Zauberberg*'s most erotic and sensual passages—I think in particular of the scene involving Hans Castorp and Madame Chaucht in the sanatorium's darkening diningroom, the two of them vibrantly up to something which doesn't ever get said.

(There is, and this looks like the place to speak of it, an enthralling, yes, story to be told in this connection. A number of years after her parents' deaths the Mann's daughter Erika placed an ad in a number of Europe's leading newspapers, asking if any reader had spent time in Venice in the same months as Thomas's and Katia's lengthiest holiday in that town, a period during which there had been a cholera outbreak both in Venice and the surrounding territory. A period, of course, which Mann made use of in his novella *Death in Venice*. An answer to Erika's ad came from a Polish count in Warsaw. The count had been a boy in his early teens that year, holidaying in Venice with his mother and sisters. He had spent every day playing with other boys on the beach at the Lido, and he remembered an elderly gentleman who had been in the habit of sitting in a deckchair on the beach reading—reading and watching him and his friends at their running and wrestling and swimming, the count's letter said. He'd been told the gentleman was a famous writer.)

The diary powerfully evokes the Munich of post-1919 Germany, those anarchic pre-Weimar months when the city, like other German towns and cities, was full of real perils and uncertainties. Bands of soldiers roamed the streets and parks, a few burghers got themselves shot, burglaries were commonplace, and Thomas and Katia sat up late in their big house and watched and listened. Thomas was filled with bitterness against the conquerors, no nationality was worse than the French, the diary lists their villainies. During this period the diary untypically goes into profounder speculations, too, e.g. on the relationship of culture and democracy, speculations which in a normal year, one feels, would have thriftily been allotted to a protagonist in one of Thomas's novels. We learn that although he is resigned to the advent of political democracy, Thomas will fight to the end against "cultural democracy". "If the German spirit is to be preserved, one must recommend the separation of cultural and national life from politics", Thomas writes; and a page later he nails this down. "We must keep everything, cultural, national, philosophical, on a plane high above…democratic utilitarianism."

It sounds very much like what soon became known as the *trahison des clercs*, the 'betrayal of the intellectuals': the abandonment of political action in favour of a concentration on the life of the mind. A mistake of consequence, of course, catastrophic in the context of Germany's history in the 1930s and what the 'clercs' stood aloof from— the barbarians whom their inactivity permitted, assisted in permitting, to take power. Not totally judgeable, though, it seems to me, in terms of what Mann probably *meant* when he spoke of "democratic utilitarianism" and of his fears concerning its effect on culture and on the 'philosophical' level of a nation's internal discourse. He knew no better than anyone else of the the Gotterdämmerung, the God's Twilight, that was coming. Too complex a matter, in any case, for this review to meddle with.

That was an unusual year in Mann's life, and an uncharacteristic journal-entry. To repeat: what will make this unwieldy volume valuable to the devotee is the everyday trivia which this austere artist reveals himself as living among and contributing to. From the self-congratulatory to the insecure, the unfair to the contrite, the paternal cliché to paternal *tendresse*. He loved his daughters more than his sons, it would appear. He took too many sleeping-pills as he got older. These are not remarkable attitudes or actions. He had the typical European intellectual's views of the U.S.—contempt before visiting it, affection after the visits. He could be smug ("Wrote in Tutti Fischer's album this morning. Satisfactorily, I felt."), cynical ("Sat with Berber who handed me a long, childish letter from a Fraülein Hoffman in St.Gall. Apparently a friend of his, or likely enough his mistress."), and doting ("spent some time at little Lisa's bedside, since she was still awake. Deep affection and great tenderness.")

I have said that the book is physically unwieldy. It is also, in an odd way, raw, as if produced in a hurry: many of the entries lack any indication of place, and although hundreds of other names appear in an index with birth-and-death dates, Thomas's own dates do not. So, shortcomings. But it's a marvellous, heavy, and yes, admittedly, unprepossessing book, stuffed with almost everything you have ever wanted to know about Thomas Mann, and knew that in his fiction he would never tell you.

Tolstoy

A *TV-Guide* "background piece" for the televised *War and Peace.*

"I hate him because he never suffers", his wife confided to her diary,
"and because he writes".

THE OBJECT OF THIS DIARY-ENTRY was Leo Nikolayevich Tolstoy; the
diarist was Sophia Alexandrovna, Countess Tolstoy; and whether the
first-given ground for Sophia's animosity was justified or not, "write"
Leo certainly did. *War and Peace* has achieved a doubtful sort of
celebrity for its length alone, 1146 pages in the edition I have at hand,
and *Anna Karenina* is almost as long. And there are other novels/
novellas, a lot of short stories, and numberless political and religious
tracts. Add the letters and journals and you have one of the least
reticent figures of the modern era.

But "never suffers"? Reading the diaries you know this for the
simplistic description it is: children sickened and died, friends turned
false, critics savaged his works, and Tolstoy mourned, sorrowed,
'suffered' through these events. Only, it seems, not enough. Because
in the midst of personal loss, the work continued. Perhaps no writer
has ever matched him in this regard: Flaubert wrote while Paris fell
to the *Boches* and while his beloved mother was dying, but at least he
had the tact to write *less*; during emotional storms he wrote sentences
and paragraphs, but not chapters and rarely even whole pages. Tolstoy
never, it seems, paused. When a son, aged five, dies of croup, he writes
in his diary, "My wife is grieving".

His *wife?*

Sophia's own comment on this diary-entry isn't known, but her
long-running accusation was that her husband used her grief as grist
for the novel-mill. It's an ancient charge against writers, one has only
to pause a moment and a dozen names queue up. Among the first-
in-line could be Scott Fitzgerald, who used Zelda's raging letters from

her several hospitalizations and incarcerations word-for-word in *Tender is the Night*, finding in those letters most of the razored accuracy which show up in Nicole's outbursts against *her* husband inside that novel. Hard to excuse, such unacknowledged, tight-lipped borrowings, hard not to judge. And yet now and then—and Tolstoy's case is one of those, depending, usually, on how you feel about the man or woman inside his story who's doing the suffering—we may feel some forgiveness, a little tolerance. Forgiveness because this particular grief-master is who he is: because his gift to us all, gift still richly accessible long after the agonies and deaths of his wife, of this or that child, of all whom he knew and who knew him, all who may have felt bitterness or rage when their first appalled reading of his freshly-published work was still going on, has triumphed over time, has left its creator's own brief span far behind and lives its vivid life still. Lives it for us. They have a special shelf in our ideal library, these stories and novels of his, a shelf all to themselves, or if the shelf is shared, then only with Shakespeare. Thomas Mann wrote of Tolstoy's voice that it was "the voice of the Russian god under the golden lime-tree". Who needs further encomia after a gorgeous image like that? I'll nevertheless mention just one more: Maxim Gorky, who knew and revered Tolstoy, said his face was "the face of an ancient stone come clear".

I have two directions to go at this point. One would be to continue the list of Sophia's accusations and laments, including the traumatic instruction from her newly-acquired husband that she read his diaries on their honeymoon. Sophia was a virgin and a dozen years younger than this wealthy aristo who during his soldiering years had been accustomed to buying women most nights of the week and recording the intimate details of those purchases (as well as of his frequent determinations to seek purity in this regard) in the diaries she spent her first days with him browsing. She "never recovered" from this, her own diary tells us: "Those readings affected our relationship forever". Another direction to head off in would be to mention his frequent bouts of depression, combined with lengthy periods of religious mania. In this latter respect he fits the sinner-saint syndrome tidily: the compulsion towards holiness led him in old age to give away, or try to give away, his entire patrimony, which, had he succeeded, would have condemned his extensive family (there were thirteen children of these two: their 'incessant' quarrelling calls for a more acrobatic adjective) to living at the level of his serfs and peasants. Here, finally, Sophie won out: she employed spies and informers and kept lawyers busy anticipating and invalidating his variously frenzied or cunning attempts at saintliness. At his death it became apparent that the Tolstoy estates, too, had played a role in defeating him: they simply were too vast, they extended over too many horizons, to be neatly disposed of.

Remains to mention one more of his myriad projects: the founding of a school-system to educate the illiterate serfs. Tolstoy's boundless energies not only led him to devise and promote such a system, but also to spend hours each day in a small building which he decreed should be a schoolhouse, and where some dozen of the local children learned to write their names and do sums. It would be good to be able to report that even one of these dozen made it into the white-collar or sub-official status, but none did. The enthusiasm probably waned as a new project loomed, a purer level of holiness beckoned. The serf children wandered back into the fields.

How striking, perhaps, in view of all this, to remember what this man accomplished, to remember how, and how deservedly, he is viewed. He is probably most readers' choice as the greatest novelist ever. In the USSR, during that state's era after his death, he was not only officially admired (the cultural apparatchiks somehow managed, though not without a number of transparent, almost comical contortions, to present him as a Marxist *pur laine)*, but was installed as the equal if not the superior of Pushkin, hitherto the leading creative artist in the language. He was the epic poet of the struggle against Napoleon, a struggle which occupies about one-third of those pages in *War and Peace*.

It's a curious one-third. Here was an invading army burning and looting and slaughtering its way across Mother Russia, led by an insatiable dictator; you would expect, then, Tolstoy's book to be an indictment of these aliens, a cry for bloody revenge, maybe even a forerunner of Ilya Ehrenburg's exhortations to the USSR's armies towards the end of the 1939-45 war ("Kill! Rape! Burn!") as these armies finally left their own soil and began to move across East Prussia and into the German *Heimat*. But no such thing. "I cannot hate the French", Tolstoy wrote, "I owe them too much of my own culture". Nor did he hate Napoleon: one outsize talent acknowledging another. And so the novel offers readers its leisurely examination of the state of mind of a French general as he contemplates the final crushing of the novelist's compatriots, and unrolls that general's battle-maps of the great encounter which will be known as Borodino—both sides given, as it were, equal time, in an atmosphere devoid of anything like the fanaticism of that century-and-a-half-later war.

It's highly ironic, really, that the Bolsheviks should have given Tolstoy this iconic status. Because when Boris Pasternak, long, long afterwards, dared to give an equally unbiased view of the Revolutionary War, in his novel *Doctor Zhivago*, his book was banned in the USSR and the Soviet culture-jackals were set upon him in every literary journal of the land. Pasternak was only emulating his master in offering his humane picture of a traumatic internal bloodletting, viewing Whites and Reds alike as humans first and partisans incidentally, haphazardly; just as Tolstoy had done with the Russians and French as they gazed at each other across the snows of Borodino. But times change.

The other great images that stay with us after *War and Peace* show, of course, Pierre Bézuhov and his generous-spirited, often inept efforts to find a good life, to reach some sort of understanding of what a man and a woman should try to do and be in this world. Out of these come the memorable images of Pierre wandering about, uncertain whether he should go forward or back, in the smoke and darkness of Borodino, a simple man loose on one of the accidental stages the world later will decide to call fateful. Or Pierre lusting after the voluptuous Hélène, even as he repeats to himself, "She's stupid, stupid….There is something nasty in the feeling she excites in me, something not legitimate." Tolstoy, holy man and satyr, revisiting old encounters. Finally it's Pierre against all the odds finding his way through that smoke and darkness to, in the last chapters, his true love Natasha. And we find Tolstoy the realist unwilling, even here, particularly here one should say, to tie the ribbon's consoling bow, to pretend he can show us an achieved happiness. Instead we watch a final scene of the two of them, Pierre and Natasha, passing a middle-aged couple's run-of-the-tundra evening, and put the book down while acknowledging that although Natasha may at one time have seemed, *did* at one time seem, a glowing, world-subduing presence in this good but confused mortal's life, love and lust and marriage and all the wisdom of a rich man's library have settled nothing finally, no more than Borodino did. Life in all its smoke and darkness and incompleteness has surged up again.

Thornton Wilder

A *TV-Guide* background piece for *Our Town*

THORNTON WILDER used to say that of all the American writers of his generation he was the only one who "didn't go to Paris". This was not strictly true—he dropped into and out of Paris often—but its implications are exact. Remembering those 1920s writers who spent the middle third, in some cases almost all, of their lives in Paris and Europe (Ernest Hemingway, Scott Fitzgerald, Gertrude Stein) there is a clear sense in which Wilder is odd man out. The simplest way to speak of this might be to invoke the slogan so often applied to those expatriates—'The Lost Generation'. Wilder may have been the least-lost major American writer of the 20th century.

His personal circumstances might have made this easy for him, certainly there are elements of the classic 'childhood of the writer' about those circumstances. His father, Amos Wilder, was a well-off Wisconsin newspaper editor, a devout Congregationalist, and as ambitious for his sons and daughters as for himself. At one point he got himself appointed consul to Hong Kong and then to Shanghai, a career that apparently ran aground on the shoals or shallows of his own egotism. At 15, Thornton was sent home from China to California, where he found himself at a boarding school more celebrated for its high standard of horseback riding than for anything he was good at. Young Wilder watched his classmates career past and guessed that if he were to excel, it would not be like this. There was a theatre nearby where he began spending his afternoons and making notes towards a first and then a second play, and from this time on, although there are shifts from California to Ohio's Oberlin College to Yale to a job teaching French in Lawrenceville, New Jersey, almost all the drama of Wilder's life is concentrated in his writings. No marriage, no children, no non-familial (he had four siblings, and they seem to have been close) relationships to report on or speculate about. There is probably no single 20th century American author whose *life* seems more bereft of significant event.

Though there was one *über*-significant event which was crucial to the years of uninterrupted work ahead: the publication in 1927 of the novel *The Bridge of San Luis Rey*. That book's not, I think, well known today, but in its time it was a bestseller, and years later it was made into a film, starring—now there's a word Wilder would curl his lip at—among others, Robert de Niro. A little-noted part of that 1927 triumph is that it became one of my mother's favourite books, which meant that I got to read it at a fairly early age. I re-read it during this past week and think it (a) more a novella than a novel— its 230 pages use a print-size designed for the hard-of-seeing; and (b) perhaps, for most of its length, the finest novella I have ever read.

What the 'Bridge' is is an extended meditation on the private histories of five people whose lives converge upon an ancient osier bridge built by the Incas, "the finest bridge in all Peru"—a convergence which occurs on a day when those osier ropes finally unravel and the five are "precipitated into the gulf below". It's written in a manner I think no one has ever quite managed to reproduce, and perhaps no one has ever tried, though as you will have gathered I think it would be worth the effort. Wilder combines here a sophistication both in language and story-development that rivals Proust but is brutally swift by comparison with that world-champion dawdler—combines this with occasional verbal naivetés which can, stumbling out of such a skill-background, startle the reader, but which serve a purpose I don't think I'd have been able to predict, let alone admire, if I hadn't found it here. By 'verbal naiveté' I mean, e.g., the use of a word like "awkwardest" ("He was the awkwardest speaker in the world") or, on a nearby page, "serener", when 'more serene' would seem to recommend itself (and not just to the finickiest, as Wilder might say, reader). Moments like these, you come to realize, keep the narrative anchored where Wilder clearly wants it to be, in a simplicity, a surface careless-ness, that saves the whole from self-consciousness and also, I think, masks its subtlety, its seldom-acknowledged high art. This continuing focus of Wilder's, this 'aesthetic', results in a story of such purity that (for whatever this may be worth) I found it, on this reading and most especially in *one* of its five 'Parts', almost literally breath-taking. Try reading the 'Part' I'm singling out here, an account of the brief lives of the twins Manuel and Esteban who were "discovered in the foundlings' basket before the door of the Convent of Santa Maria de la Rosas" in Lima. And then try (though why should you?), when you've finished it, *not* to take a long pause in your thoughts of anything *other than* these two luminously-conceived, deeply moving, bare-of-a-single-wasteful-syllable lives.

It's interesting, I think, to look at the sort of style-decision I've just mentioned and realize how close it comes to the essential voice of *Our Town*, surely Wilder's riskiest and most memorable play. For a lot of people it's responsible for their sense of Wilder as a cracker-barrel philosopher, folksy apologist for the status quo. And in fact there's a remark of his own which seems to bear this out, and which has been much quoted by those anxious to make an understandable but ultimately, I think, unhingedly simplistic point. "I would love to be the poet of Coney Island", is the remark. Wilder did indeed say this, although he said it, I believe, only once. A careful reading of his works will show just how complex and subtle a claim for love this was.

Edward Munch

Visual Arts pages, *The Globe and Mail*

I FIRST SAW EDVARD MUNCH's paintings in two of Stockholm's major galleries when I lived in that city for a few years in the late 1950s. I remember being puzzled that so many of this Norwegian's central works should have their home in Stockholm rather than in his own country—especially since , in that postwar decade, relations were pretty frosty between Sweden, the wartime neutral and profiteer, and Norway, the wartime occupied and oppressed.

Well, of course the answer was that almost every one of Munch's best-known paintings exists in a number of versions: different canvas-sizes, different materials, woodcuts, lithographs, sketches, etc., all of the same image. Almost identical versions of his *Sick Child*, his *Girls on a Bridge*, his *Melancholy*, and of course his *Madonna*, are findable in more than one gallery in more than one town. And being near the source, no surprise that the Swedes have a bunch of them.

This repetition of a motif is obviously not unique to Munch, but in his case we pretty well know what was going on. It turns out that Munch had this peculiar idea—no, these two peculiar ideas. The first was that the true artist should paint not what his eyes saw, but what his soul saw. That's what he said, and what he seems to have meant was that any painting of his should show what was being registered by the deepest-down and simplest and most naïve and naked piece of inner apparatus he had. And the second and related idea was that if the artist did this, and did it obstinately and continuously— reworking the same image over and over until it reached its most primal level—then something very new and real about what it is to be human might be communicated to anybody who was willing to take an unhurried look.

Munch's wish was that a gallery would hang as many of his works as its walls could take. Ideally, the gallery would show everything he'd ever done: the major things of course, but also the minors: sketches, written scrawls beneath or above or in the margins of a sketch…the lot. He felt that the record of a soul's progression through a life, displayed unconditionally and meticulously, nothing withheld, could reach and move and change those who saw it, and do this in a way and to a degree that no individual painting could do. This sounds like Rainer Maria Rilke's famous account of a poem's injunction to its readers: read me, and having done so, understand that you must change your life. Munch never said that, or anything really close to it, so far as I know. But it is implicit in his view of his art. And what drew me, there in Stockholm, to Munch's stark and, in a very obvious sense, unsubtle paintings was just that—their starkness and unsubtlety; the power of these images which so blatantly kept focusing on things as elemental and elementary as loneliness, death, solitude, beauty, the torments and yearnings of sex, the stillness of a summer evening by a lake.

Part of the reason for its effect on me was very probably that I was meeting these images in a decade dominated by Modernism, Eliot, Pound, Picasso, and many a *semblable*—poets and painters for whom things were anything but elemental, anything but raw. Wherever you looked , in those days, you saw subtlety, complexity, masks under masks, a "continual extinction of personality", as Eliot advised (they weren't all really doing that, the writers and artists, but they said they were, and most of their critics and spokespeople believed them or said they did, and it's funny how that affects the way books get read and art gets looked at). By contrast, Munch's images seemed, on the one hand, so unambiguous as to be not merely simple but simple-minded, cartoonish—where was the mind-challenge here?—but on the other hand—

Well, on the other hand, his images were deeply moving. Yes. And more and more so as you kept on looking, as you went back for second and third looks.

Needless to say it's that 'other-hand' that has lasted. Ten years later, when my acquired Swedish allowed me to read enough Norwegian to get by, I spent a week in the cellars of Oslo's Munch Museum reading his untranslated (they're still mostly un-Englished; more of them, though far from all of them, can be read in German) diaries.

The same head-on, uncomplicated, sometimes angry, always direct voice was speaking there. The words were no rival to Munch's paint, to the shapes and colours on his canvases, but their honesty was appealing, often touching. Munch was, I now think, in his willingness to keep on exploring his feelings, his 'soul', and his willingness, also, to send out messages of what he was finding, similar to a few, but only a few, other artists and writers of his time. They didn't call themselves 'Expressionists' but many of them have been, matter of convenience, called that in the fifty-odd years since. Käthe Köllwitz is an easy choice, for one. Thomas Hardy is a less easy choice and has, I'll guess, never been called that and nor should he, but there is a clear connection between Hardy (in his poetry, which was all he really valued about his own writings) and Munch: neither of them put up any defences against clarity, against being understood. They both thought that love and death and a few other things that nobody really can ignore or escape were what needed to be talked about, or shown, or struggled with, and they both wanted as many people as possible to know these thoughts of theirs. They both speak to what a nearer-contemporary of ours, the poet Philip Larkin, was describing when he offered his opinion that here and there, unpredictably but surely, "someone will forever be surprising/ A hunger in himself to be more serious". It's this, I think, that enabled Edvard Munch's work to survive the almost unremitting hostility, the fury, the demonizing, of his own lifetime. It may even help it to survive the million reproductions of his 'Madonna' and the stick-on buttons and inflatable plastic dollies of his 'Scream' of *our* lifetimes.

Frye

The Correspondence of Northrop Frye and Helen Kemp 1932-1939; in two volumes, edited by Robert Denham

HEFTING THESE two substantial books before opening them, I admit to suspecting that what we had here was probably an over-pious *hommage* to The Great Man. Could the seven-year correspondence of two very young persons, Northrop and Helen, respectively 20 and 22 when it begins, possibly be worth these near-thousand pages, these several years (four, Denham tells us) of an editor's time, these many annotations, and finally these one hundred and forty dollars?

Baseless suspicion, it turns out. The Great Man—and there's no irony in this reviewer's use of the phrase—triumphs over the forbidding appearance of these two tomes, triumphs also over the footnoted format, over his own youth and a pretty funny hairdo—triumphs through the sheer unremitting shining-forth of his wit, his impatience, and his clear promise of what's to come. In short, the books document the early years of an unmistakable and close-to-unique intelligence.

Strong words. I think there will hardly be a student of those times—those undergraduate and graduate English courses and that celebrated course known as 'RK', Religious Knowledge—who will disagree with them.

Denham's editing is in most of the critical areas admirable. His introductions to the various sections (years and seasons) are managed with economy, modesty and an increasingly trustable sensitivity. He provides links and synopses of events which the letters haven't dealt with, and then he gets out of the light. The index is good.

My only caveat isn't a large one. Some of the many footnotes are of a sort that not even the least demanding of browsers will require, e.g. *The Magic Flute* is footnoted "an opera by Mozart." When, in one of her letters, Helen decides she's getting a touch verbose and preachy, she adds, "Whoa there, Polonius!", and the footnote crunches in with "That is, she should stop herself from issuing advice like the sententious mentor in Shakespeare's *Hamlet*". These are not good moments but they are in very small print.

One of the distinctive pluses of the correspondence is that Frye—a highly private man, a man who never seemed able to engage his students in the sort of small-talk that might have led to a personal revelation or two, a man about whose off-podium life very little was known, although much was sought for—is shown here with all the undefended openness of a young scholar, a young minister in a Saskatchewan summer mission field, and, above all, a young lover.

Helen comes through as, among other things that I'll get to, intelligent and vulnerable. She fails her exams at the Courtauld Institute of Art in London, and offers to step out of his life: "I will not have you marry a stupid woman" (her 23-year-old lover deals with the offer firmly and with a touching tenderness). She is also loyal to her friends. When Norrie takes a few shots at Kathleen Coburn, for whom he has little scholarly respect and no personal liking at all—"the Coburn bitch"—this is what he gets by return of post: "And don't call Kay Coburn names—I told you she is a good friend of mine, and I stick to it. You needn't be rude." Norrie apologizes in a hurry.

There are dozens, hundreds, of surprises in these letters, not least concerning the very close, very mutually dependent nature of this love affair and the early years of the marriage. Cries of loneliness from each to the other during their frequent separations, explicit and witty descriptions of sexual longing, with each playing her or his characteristic role. Helen writes to NF, who is by now at Merton College in Oxford, of a dream in which a gorilla pursues and partly disrobes her. By return of post NF assures her that when he gets back "you will find yourself with even fewer clothes than the gorilla left you." These are comforting things to know about both of them.

Comforting, too, to find them both behaving in some respects just like everybody else. Like, for instance, awakening a little jealousy during these long separations. Helen mentions in a half-dozen letters the assorted former swains who are still hanging about; one of these apparently gives her a frat pin, which as I recall used to be not quite but almost the equivalent of an engagement ring. Nothing more is heard of the frat pin, apparently Norrie didn't rise to the bait, or if he did he was cool about it. He does, it's true, mention that a one-time girlfriend is in the neighbourhood when he's back visiting in Moncton, and there's a suggestion that somebody or other when he's at Merton has paid him some notice, but the sport doesn't really engage him and he's soon swimming back again towards William Blake.

Ah yes, Blake. A bit skewed, you may have been thinking, to do a review of anything touching Northrop Frye without focusing even at this stage on the scholarship, the brainy young grad-student trying out early and occasionally startling judgments on books from *The Whiteoaks of Jalna* ("a beautiful book") to Wyndham Lewis's *Apes of God* ("probably the best English novel since *Ulysses*, if that is in English").

I'm going to trust my feeling, though, that since rather a lot is known about *Fearful Symmetry* and the lengthy shelf of titles that followed, this review is better off staying with Helen and Norrie and their profound mutual affection. I'll end with the opening of a 1935 letter addressed to Helen in London, her year at the Courtauld.

> "My dear Helen:
> "What a completely redundant expression that invocation is! Still, I don't know—it's a sort of trinity. 'My'—that's you in your subjective aspect; "Helen'—that's you in your objective, individual aspect; 'dear'—that's the *copula*, or link connecting us. There ought to be one word for it all, though, to save wear and tear on the space bar."

You'll be glad to know that he then starts over with, "Sweetheart."

Théatre national populaire*

JEAN VILAR's Popular National Theatre (T.N.P. to the French, who tend to put many things backward, so that even NATO sounds like that unlucky thane in *Beowulf*) is at the Palace Theatre in London, where it is doing fair business before a mostly émigré house. This group has no counterpart here, which is England's bad luck—its productions are by far the most exciting in Paris, and among other good things it has brought about is the shock-awakening of the Comédie, which was deeply asleep and passing the time like a Cocteau candelabra-head stoney-eyeing Racine, etc (Racine will probably survive, but I have cheerful forebodings about Corneille). The T.N.P.'s London plays are Hugo's *Marie Tudor,* Marivaux's *Le Triomphe de l'Amour,* and Molière's *Don Juan*—a typically mixed bag, and no evening is without its good things. It's too bad about the playhouse, though: the Palace is not strictly on Shaftesbury Avenue, which cuts it off from that most dependable of box-office equations, i.e., nobody sidles in by mistake.

In spite of all this the Marivaux's first night was what its title promised, a triumph. The play is in the French tradition of delicate, stylised comedy, and it was delicately choreographed and acted, with Maria Casarès as the princess who makes various love to persons of all the sexes in order to finally hone in on the one she wants. It is a deliberately mannered performance which does not sacrifice the character to the personality of this classical actress—her voice and movements are like clear water within which Leonide, the Princess, is still and perfect and unharassed, and recognizably Marivaux. Daniel Sorano as Arlequin has a good shot at Colette Marchand as Fernandel.

Atmosphere aside, it must be nice for Maria Casarès to abandon Lady Macbeth *("va! va! tâche maudite!"),* Cocteau's *Les Parents Terribles*, and other such melos for a role like this.

What *Marie Tudor* is like on the smaller Palace stage I can't say; on their own ground, at the Palais de Chaillot, it is that blurbish phrase, a magnificent spectacle. Draped drums, hooded executioners bearing immense papier-mâché axes and leading other hooded and bound figures to the block, the Casarès again, and a curtain line which suddenly brings another whole dimension into the mind (like a subterranean stage rising, on which an even more dramatic play has been darkly going forward): this is more than any currently fashionable playwright can offer casually.

The *Don Juan* isn't of this class, Jean Vilar makes a better director than actor on this showing. The actor lived upstage the performance I saw, and he seemed often, that night, to be mistaking movement for action and effusiveness for emotion. That was my one and only night watching him, I'd better say. But anyway, *Don Juan…?*

*This is what I think and hope is an anomaly: a review written when I was an undergraduate at Cambridge and one which, because I was young enough not to know better, I'm prepared to acknowledge as mine. It appeared in *The Broadsheet*, a cyclostyled publication marked, I notice, "price Threepence" and edited by a friend of mine called Michael Boddy. I was just back from my second summer on the continent, hence my expertise in the French classical theatre.

D.M. Thomas

Sphinx by D.M. Thomas (review in *The London Review of Books*)

THERE ARE MANY THOMASES in the field of letters and I must declare an interest in this one. The interest is not benign. Dylan, R.S., Edward—these three Thomases I to varying degrees admire, respect, applaud. I would rather have tramped the English counties with Edward than with any other poet.

Than with any other man, I will go so far as to say.

With D.M., however, I have had no luck at all.

Our relationship began with the publication some years ago of *The Flute Player*, a novel which, I had heard, concerned the life of Osip Mandelstam. Mandelstam was and is, for me, the purest of 20th-century poets; even in English his lines meet my eyes with an unsurpassed directness. His wife Nadezhda wrote in one of her two fine books about her husband, "You always know when you are reading a true poem—there is a feeling which cannot be mistaken", and I've always been struck by the resemblance between this and St. Teresa of Avila's news for her readers concerning the means by which we can distinguish the voice of God from that of the Devil: "There is an authority, an immediate and unmistakable conviction, when the true voice speaks". True voice, true poem—and no possibility of mistaking either when you hear it or read it. As far as the 'true poem' goes, I have thought and still think, yes, this is so. And, feeling that Osip Mandelstam left hardly anything untrue among the poems that survived Stalin's panting, remorseless, half-successful huntings-down of his work (a legacy no one else has, I think, quite rivalled), when I heard about *The Flute Player* there was no chance I'd not buy it and read it, buy it without even a browse or a check on its reviews. A rash move on my part, and the beginning of the unlucky relationship mentioned above; a relationship which has only become more perplexing as Thomas's reputation has, as it undoubtedly has, grown.

Here's what I found in that novel. A mix of fragments of poetry, the gratuitous naming of admired names, a collage of superficially evoked 'real' events and persons, the whole of this in a bath of embarrassingly banal dialogue which masked or tried to mask its clichés by offering them now in French, now in Russian, now in yet another non-English tongue—and all of it rushed past the reader's eye so swiftly that it reminded me of nothing so much as my old teacher Marshall McLuhan at his rapid-fire worst, evading ordinary folks' plain questions by ping-ponging back little tags from Valéry, Gide, St.Augustine or whoever came into his mind, keeping things moving, now-I'm-serious-now-I'm-not, terrific, class over. The comparison between McLuhan and Thomas should not be carried too far, though. Quite a lot of the time McLuhan was brilliant.

The only passages that slowed Thomas down were the leisurely voyeuristic ones, the scannings of bodies engaged in close-focus sex; a special-interest area for him, as I've since discovered, and by no means unusual in our supermarket paperbacks. But this was a novel which purported to have some connection with the work and life of Osip Mandelstam, a man so clarity-ridden that his lines and images seem to have arrived on the page by the simplest of all conceivable routes, leaving nothing for the reader to do with them or about them forever except to gaze and be reminded of a series of possibilities as near-to-the-mind's-core as anything he or she has imagined.

And a man of a notable privacy and discretion, in his life as in his work.

It was puzzling, but not *that* puzzling, after all. Exploitation comes, as everybody knows, in infinite varieties. This was one of them. End of my relationship with this particular bearer of the Thomas name, why not.

Two reasons why not. The first was the success, runaway variety, of a later book of his, *The White Hotel*. The second was this present offering, *Sphinx*. After everyone else had read *The White Hotel* I read it too, found it as bogus as I was sure it would be, and still find the praise it was given incomprehensible. In Britain a reviewer described Thomas as "a profound myth-maker", a description I'd have thought could be corrected if the reviewer valued the word 'profound' at all, to say nothing of getting straight the difference between myth-making and myth-exploiting.

The White Hotel purports to show Freud at work, it surprises F. in a number of pocket-torch-lit sequences (reading and writing letters, mostly), there are glimpses of the potent and yes, mythic Freudian nightscape here and there. But the relationship of novel to myth is neither creative nor illuminating, it is parasitic. The fancy footwork is as adroit as ever, the mix of history and fiction is still in place, the deflections away from every apparently-imminent clarity continue; and the reliance on sadomasochistic sex, already visible in *The Flute Player*, is by now extreme. By the way, I have come to the conclusion that the unwillingness of critics to take on this aspect of Thomas's work has a lot to do with his slippery technique. He tends to present these sexual pay-offs in doggerel verse—a facile literary mode, after all, but one which I've noticed reviewers in the U.K. show a weird degree of respect for (*viz.* the ubiquitous showings-up in prestigious journals of the verse of Tony Harrison); and when Thomas gets himself really dug into these scenes there's a noticeably crude use of simile, of metaphor, of sheer unsubtle juxtaposition.

> that night he almost burst my cunt apart
> being tighter from my flow of blood, the stars
> were huge over the lake, there was no room
> for a moon, but the stars fell in our room.

Thomas likes this mind-numbing balderdash a lot, both the verse-form, which more often than not rhymes, and the content here. He likes it more with each book, it seems.

Finally to *Sphinx*. It's the third in a sequence, 'linked but independent', and for purposes of this review I've now conscientiously read the other two. This one has three central characters, the poet Rozanov, the *Guardian* 'journalist' Lloyd George, and the sphinx herself, Nadia, who is certainly an actor and a beauty and may also be a KGB agent. Much talk of *improvisatore*, suspenders, the Pushkin Museum of Fine Arts, small or big tits, Akhmatova, Isadora Duncan, small or big tits, suspenders, small or…etc. "I asked him if he didn't think it was slightly immoral, mixing reality and fiction", one character confides, and inside Thomas's text the subversive query is triumphantly squashed ("the trouble with most novels…one knew they weren't true, and therefore they were boringly irrelevant").

The techniques familiar from the earlier novels are all present here, the only difference being that Thomas has grown careless and everything's even more blatant. Foreign words and phrases have multiplied, though in their obtrusive knowingness they endear themselves no more than they did before. We learn that Finns, in orgasmic moments, cry "Hääyöaie!", and in case we've missed anything the ingenuous journalist George asks "Is that really the Finnish word for orgasm?" and is assured that yes, it is. Why Finns should cry out a word with three umlauts while experiencing it, as a couple of them repeatedly do in the next-door railway compartment, is a further question I wish George had asked.

More than a quarter of the text is in verse, some of it in rhyming couplets ('Thatcher' is twice rhymed with 'dacha', 'Dürer' with *nomenklatura*) and some of the scenes involving the omniseductive Nadia with the 'ageing confidant' of a Polish Pope are, I'm altogether ready to admit, very funny. True that the comic effect is unintentional and doesn't jibe with the narrative at any of these points, but that's the way it goes.

Here are a few late examples of the slapdash invoking (and whether this is condescension on Thomas's part or merely stiff-wittedness I leave it to you to decide) of a supposedly-shared intellectual *niveau*. A trivial conversation in a railway car produces, "I thought of a phrase in *Whitsun Weddings*….this frail travelling coincidence", and Thomas can't leave this without nailing it down, without having the reliable George interpolate "by my favourite poet Larkin". It's George, again, who meets a tottery couple who confess how out of place they feel, and pat on its cue comes, as you knew it would, "This is no country for old men" followed by "as Yeats had put it". The third-from-last page comes up with "Nothing, almost, is a surprise/ The Sphinx is moving his slow thighs."* And the name Nadezhda (which *means* hope) prompts the same *lumpen* lummox to "hope against hope."**

Small wonder that nobody's named as the editor of rubbish like this.

---

*The "moving…slow thighs" is of course Yeats again; Thomas must have decided to keep shut about this one.
**The title of Nadezhda Mandelstam's first and best book.

Ruskin

John Ruskin: The Later Years by Tim Hilton

WHAT A GOLDEN AGE this is for literary biography! Back from whatever disregard they have been idling in, rubbing their eyes, come the fresh-wakened heroes of other times—William Morris, Pushkin, Coleridge, Ruskin, and closer-to-us names too, Camus, Beckett (twice in one year) and Woolf. The news about most of these, not to be shy about it, is wonderful—these are lives to read and to have your mind new-stocked and your heart uplifted by.

I've been reading Tim Hilton's art criticism in *The Guardian* for years, so his was a trusted name. He doesn't disappoint. *John Ruskin: The Later Years* is the second of a two-volume life of one of the most monolithic of the Stonehenge-proportioned Victorians—and it's just as stupendous in research and intelligence as Volume one was. (Yes, *The Early Years*).

Ruskin is 40 when this one begins, and his father has only five years to live. That father, John James Ruskin, as a young man had longed for a life in art, but he had a living to earn. He did that, he made a fortune in the wine-importing business, and then he more or less deposited that fortune, *carte blanche*, into his son's account. It was far from the only offering that this adoring father made to his son. Having satisfied himself that John Jr. had both manners and talent, he thenceforth retreated from any reproof or criticism, assisted with joy and deference in the accumulation of the most extensive collection of the paintings of J.M.W. Turner anywhere (his money, of course), and uttered not a whisper when, without consultation and knowing full well that his father loved those paintings with a passion equal to his own, the son later sold them off—doing this almost, it seems, to erase the evidence of a unique generosity.

That may be the worst news, maybe the second-worst, you will hear about the younger Ruskin in this book. All the rest is heartening, almost awe-inspiring. Grown up, he was celebrated for his energies, his idealism, his genius. He "had a way of calling an audience to vast and intangible tasks", Hilton writes, a lovely judgment. His industry was unceasing. There was a monthly newsletter called *Fors Clavigera* which the entire literate citizenry, you feel, subscribed to and arranged their lives and travels such that no single issue would escape them. There are the famous books: *The Stones of Venice, Sesame and Lilies, Modern Painters.* He was the first Professor of Art at Oxford and annoyed the dons with his casual attitude toward lecturing, annoying them again by being so popular that he had to deliver each lecture twice, lest the hundreds queuing outside riot.

He repaid the dons' dislike in full. Describing a Carpaccio painting he'd recently seen in Italy, Ruskin said that the gathering of scholars pictured by Carpaccio could be likened to "a complete assembly of highly trained Oxford men as far as expression went; but with more brains."

But he squandered John James's lovingly testamented money (in today's terms, millions of pounds), bestowing it now wisely and now merely self-indulgently, his erratic behaviour puzzling the well-intentioned as often as it exasperated the pompous.

And then there's this other thing—Ruskin and women. It's a curious matter, but one which I don't feel inclined to mock, all these starry 19th-century English gents (Dodgson/Carroll, Carlyle, Ruskin), idealists, social reformers, artists and poets…so many of them with dubious credentials in matters sexual. Ruskin famously was so taken aback to learn, on his and Effie's wedding night, that his unclothed bride did not resemble the airbrushed nudes of classical sculpture (i.e. that she had pubic hair) that he never got over it. (As for Effie, once she got the hang of things with another partner, she was almost permanently pregnant). And time doesn't improve the story. There was a years-long infatuation with a very young Irish girl, the splendidly named Rose La Touche, and several dozen schoolgirls after Rose.

It needs to be said, though, that none of these, as far as any public-or-other-spirited inquiry has managed to establish, were touched, none fondled, and no hoard of indiscreet daguerrotypes has ever turned up. An unalloyed dream, it seems to have been, a dream of 'pure' companionship such as adolescence often has, or used to have, but normally awakens from. Nothing enviable about it, plenty that's pitiable, but not much, if you ask me, that's judgeable.

A very minor complaint: Hilton might have given us less of the prolonged and repetitive descriptions of the intermittent "madness" leading towards Ruskin's death in 1900—it's a kind of behaviour that surely sounds very familiar to our Alzheimer-accustomed hearing. Whatever the illness was, a stream of friends, disciples and persons he had succoured years or even decades before, kept arriving to beg him not to die. Not the worst kind of farewell for that brilliant, inspiring, confused mind.

Hilton's two-volume report on that mind should pre-empt the field for a good while. The sheer hard work that goes into books like these makes some of our critical snobberies and categories look silly. And when the research surfaces in prose of this quality, then it merits the encomium "work of art" very much more than, I think, is the case with a thousand or two of this or any year's novels and poetry-collections.

Dylan Thomas

Dylan Thomas: A New Life by Andrew Lycett

'HOW CAN WE KNOW the dancer from the dance?' a better poet than the one whose life is recorded here wrote, and in Dylan Thomas's case the answer's easy. *Dancer*: a sponging, cheating, pugnosed drunk, vomiting his way through a brief life married to a ditto woman. (Caitlin outlived him by 40 years, spending some of those years on Elba, where the villagers shouted "*prostituta*" after her when she emerged from her boozy nights with one or another local fisherman). *Dance*: some of the most celebrated lines written in English in the 20th century.

There's nothing unique about this, of course. Poets behave badly, or at least male poets do. This is generally understood: from Christopher Marlowe to Robert Lowell and many before, after, and in between, drink and women (and other genres and genders) do them in, and if they mostly belong under the 'brief lives' rubric, well, so much the better, not nice to have known them. Dylan Thomas died at 39 in New York, officially of pneumonia, in fact of two decades of near-incessant drinking. His last night on this earth he had been at a party during which he had "made a fool of himself" by chasing a young girl around the room. This is forgivable only until you read that (according to his first biographer, John Malcolm Brinnin), "he was so violent that the young girl suffered a concussion".

Well, I'm not going to get into the overworked issue of what Art justifies and what Nothing At All justifies. It's an interesting issue but no, not today.

What I will do is tell you that this latest Thomas Biography is lengthy and, being lengthy, doesn't leave much out. There's a table showing the family trees of both Dylan and Caitlin, and those trees start in the 18th century, which strikes me as a little early. Neither family seems ever to have distinguished itself, unless you count the degree of dysfunction a family can attain, which in Dylan's case was extreme. His father , a sour Swansea schoolmaster known as D.J., was given to muttering "throw the little bugger out" when baby Dylan caused any sort of ruckus, and the same charmer once threw a book at Dylan's sister while informing her, "It's a pity you're alive".

This is all too bad, and much sympathy goes to those two children, but British writer Andrew Lycett can't leave it alone. Granted what's coming, I mean the grimy behaviour the next generation's going to regale us with, I'd have thought it a better idea if Lycett had got on his horse towards the good stuff, the poems, much sooner than he did. We all know that the poems are the only reason we're here, and Lycett's trudging prose isn't notable enough, his mind's just not well-stocked enough, to quieten our drumming fingers.

So enough of the life, the 'dancer'. The poems now, that's different—things incandesce as soon as we reach them. They're not *all* marvels, nobody's are unless your name is Shakespeare, but eight or nine of them will probably make it into succeeding editions of the *Oxford Book of English (sic) Verse* forever, and they'll deserve every page they get.

Returning to these poems after years away, I found things I'd never noticed before, for example powerful echoes of Shakespeare in a poem beginning, "Especially when the October wind/ With frosty fingers punishes my hair", or of Joyce in, "Altarwise by owl-light in the halfway-house…". And these are minor plusses when one reaches the great and, I believe, everlasting masterworks such as *Poem in October* ("It was my thirtieth year to heaven/ Woke to my hearing"), *Fern Hill* ("Now as I was young and easy under the apple boughs"), or the finale of that same poem ("Time held me green and dying,/ Though I sang in my chains like the sea"), or the stripped-down and finally unanswerably quiet beauty of *In My Craft Or Sullen Art*.

There is something to be said, you know, for writing lines that millions more people know and love than ever stray near to the skinny bookcases, fatally identified as Poetry, in our libraries and bookshops—lines that move readers, that have a depth to them, a depth that people can look into and actually see things they recognize or remember or find mysterious or beautiful. There are only a very, very few 20th century poets writing in English who gave us such lines,

Philip Larkin and Theodore Roethke were the most recent of them and before those two there was Edward Thomas and Thomas Hardy and A.E.Housman and Yeats; and the only other one who makes it into that loved, yes, list as far as I'm concerned, is Dylan Thomas, this unattractive little Welshman. He didn't last long and didn't leave a quarter as many poems as, say, Hardy left, but among the poems he left are some of the most-quoted lines of his century, lines that didn't go with him when he went, they stayed right here where we all still are. "Do not go gentle into that good night/ Rage, rage, against the dying of the light"—those two lines are, Lycett tells us, on thousands of gravestones. So is a lot of sad doggerel, you will say. Sure, but among that doggerel can appear unexpected shinings, and lines like these will always stop us for a minute or two in our desultory Sunday wanderings.

Having begun with such a black picture of him, I need to close with a personal anecdote. Thomas came to Cambridge during my first year there, to read at the Union, and a friend of mine, a married American graduate student who had the misfortune to have a house with an extra bedroom, was asked to put the visiting poet and notorious vomiter-cum-violator up for the night. My friend worried mightily over this, but finally agreed. What else could he do?

Thomas showed up, went off to read, came back late but so quietly nobody heard him come in, and was down for breakfast smelling of nothing worse than aftershave. Talk about disappointment.

Hugo

Victor Hugo: A Biography by Graham Robb

UNTIL I READ Graham Robb's book, I took it as a given that no modern European writer had so dominated the life and letters of his country as Leo Tolstoy did throughout a very long life in Russia. Or, failing, him, Goethe. Even though what has become Germany was in those years divided into a patchwork of princedoms, the Sage of Weimar's influence was felt everywhere his language was spoken, and well beyond that too. Surely it was one of those two.

Not so, it seems. If Goethe's *Werther* put him at the age of 24 on a map he would never leave, Victor Hugo's early odes won him a pension from the King of France at 21. If a huge nation came to a stop when Tolstoy died at the age of 82 in that rustic railway station, Hugo sat at his window chipper as ever on his 80th birthday, watching a half-million Parisians file past in his honour and listening to no fewer than, apparently, 5,000 musicians trying to keep to the same tempo with the "Marseillaise".

All of which has nothing to do with quality, of course, with these men's good or bad books. It's here that things get a little complicated. Leaving the other two colossi on their unrockable daises, sticking to my assignment from now on, what complicates any judgment on Hugo is the ambivalent but richly flavoured nature of the comments left by his French contemporaries, also by their after-comers. Baudelaire, no gentle critic, said of Hugo's poetry that it was "full of beauties and stupidities". Flaubert, frightening perfectionist, said (and if you read this quotation carefully, you may feel that Flaubert is cleverly sidestepping making any sort of strictly lit-crit comment) that he would "rather talk with Hugo than with anyone".

The hands-down winner, though, is André Gide. Asked who his favourite poet was, he marvellously replied, "*Victor Hugo, hélas.*"

Comments such as these suggest what is probably a widely-held view of this protean writer: that he was, yes, prolific and gifted, but uneven, a near-genius and flag-bearer for French Romanticism who was also capable of the most overblown and commonplace work. The man who initiated the most celebrated of French literary riots, filling the Paris streets with his exotically-costumed youthful supporters after the violent opening night of his play *Hernani* (there are wonderful anecdotes about this; his 'classicist' opponents petitioned the King asking that all such Romantic plays be banned from the *Comédie Française*; to which *Le Figaro* responded by saying that this would be like "demanding a monopoly on sending audiences to sleep". And again: one of Hugo's chief tormentors was a poet named Viennet, author of what seems to have been a stupendously dull 30,000-line epic, of which a vengeful Hugoist said, "It would take 15,000 people to read it".) Hugo also, as we know, wrote *Notre-Dame de Paris* (he hated the English translation's title, *The Hunchback of Notre Dame*) and *Les Misérables*, and thousands of pages of essays, political tracts and stories, as well as hundreds and hundreds of poems.

A god during his lifetime, Hugo has not fared well with posterity. Robb, in his workman-like biography (enlivened every now and then by a sentence, involuntary I am sure, which only Sam Goldwyn or Casey Stengel could rival) thinks this is unjust. It's understandable enough, Robb allows, that critics should want to distance themselves from all that adulation (those crowds, that oversized orchestra), easy enough to note the grotesqueries in the plots, to find those entwined skeletons of Quasimodo and Esmerelda in the catacombs of Notre Dame a bit much. But a more careful attention to the *oeuvres complètes* should, Robb suggests, bring redress, a belated fairness.

This does not seem too much to ask. Having been, as a teenager, more lastingly affected by Jean Valjean, Javert, Cosette, et al, than I ever was by, say, Sydney Carton, for the purposes of this review I went back to Hugo's most celebrated work (it was also necessary to go back behind the musical) to see how much was there that might add up to more than a cleverly-plotted, padded-up historical novel. I did not reread all of it, but long passages here and there : Fantine, wanderyears, death of Javert. Reader, it is not Mann or Musil, it is also not Eliot or Austen, but it is a long way superior to Grisham or what's-his-name, that other fellow. The energy of many of these pages, the sudden starry metaphors—dozens of these from a level far beyond average reach—and, of course, the driving story, its steadfast protagonist…there's no need for condescension here, it seems to me. Respect, rather, and a small rush of pleasure that those teenage hours of mine had been spent, after all, in good company.

Among the shorter plays, too—what Robb calls playlets—there are some interesting discoveries, including one about a 100-year-old woman in a sack. Samuel Beckett read everything that French literature offered; he may have read this, too. Sparks fly from poems, from stories, even from the corrosive political writings, of which the devastatingly-titled *Napoleon-le-Petit* was probably the most effective. Directed against the embarrassing Napoleon the Third, it was translated everywhere and hawked in all the principal Paris thoroughfares, and was probably worth an army or two in overthrowing the dictator.

Scarcely space now for the life, which was no less absorbing to Hugo's public than his writings. Marriage at a youthful age to Adèle, the courtship a torrent of poems; later the poems are for Juliette, a sometime actress and model for popular erotic sculptures, which Hugo would have seen in as many homes as we nowadays see Picasso's Quixote on his horse. Both these women loved him all their long lives; at the age of 60 Adèle published a biography of her husband, and Juliette wrote him a love letter every morning for fifty years. Besides those two, there were about a thousand others, servant girls, translators, groupies *avant la letter*. He lived in exile for almost twenty years, most of these in the Channel Islands. He and Adèle had five children, and the waltz-music dies away, the smiles are wiped off reading faces, when we come to them. Hostages to talent, is what is usually said at this point.

Victor Hugo died in 1885 at the age of 83. The crush of the funeral crowds pushed a woman off a bridge to drown in the Seine, together with a man who tried to save her. Someone else in the crowd gave birth. The hero was buried in the Pantheon, where later, Emile Zola, who hated him, would lie beside him.

Brecht

Brecht & Co.: Sex, Politics and the Making of the Modern Drama
by John Fuegi

THE LAST 20 *anni* have been pretty *horribili* for Bertolt Brecht's reputation. His plays have faded offstage, his leftwing credentials have been called into question, his personal life qualifies as seriously bad news, in general his enemies have been noisily outshouting his supporters. Indeed it's hard to know where to look for the latter nowadays. In the book *Intellectuals*, published a few years ago, Paul Johnson subtitled his Brecht chapter *Heart of Ice* and quoted Auden as calling BB "an odious person". Brecht deserved the death sentence, Auden said, and added, "In fact I can imagine doing it to him myself."

Woo-ee. Brecht must have gone white as a sheet.

But the chorus goes on. Thomas Mann, Theodor Adorno (who said Brecht spent hours every day putting dirt under his fingernails so he'd look like a worker), Marcuse, almost every known German contemporary and many more who are neither German nor contemporary, the judgment's just about unanimous—flawed writer, flawed man. And rather worse than that, as you're about to find out.

To this list must now be added the name of the author of the swollen object under review here. It's 732 pages of near-unrelenting Brecht-bashing, so many charges of plagiarism, deceit, the coldhearted sexual and professional manipulation of co-workers both female and male, that either as man or as artist it seems Brecht's got nowhere to hide. Literally nowhere. You'd think the shower-stall would be safe, but you'd be wrong: even in matters of personal hygiene, this book tells you, BB was somebody you didn't want to stand too near.

Well it's clear that most of this is true and that a lot of it needed saying, and a bit more of it will be said in this review. Not, though, before I mention that I think it's pretty odd to learn, from this book's dust-jacket, that its author is "the founder of the International Brecht

Society and managing editor of fourteen volumes of its pro-ceedings…also the editor of *The Essential Brecht*", etc.

Leaves one feeling a touch bemused, that does.

But on with the story. We learn here that one of Brecht's lovers, Elizabeth Hauptmann, wrote most of *The Threepenny Opera*, and that large portions of almost every other play involved the collaboration, at the very least, of other women in the Brecht circle (Grete Steffin, Ruth Berlau, Helene Weigel). BB's casualness in appropriating (read: plagiarizing) the work of others was apparently remarkable even for those irregular times. An excerpt from a cabaret skit by the splendid satirist Kurt Tucholsky (who by the way *was* splendid; he's easily my favourite of the pre-war Berlin cabaret entertainers, of whom, luckily, written records exist; he also wrote a likeably sexy novella, *à la* Laurence Sterne, of travels with his mistress in Sweden; and the last thing to say of him right now is that he was Jewish, as so many of the Berlin intelligentsia were, and that he committed suicide in Sweden during his Nazi-enforced exile there) illustrates this: a character asks, "Who is the play by?", and the reply comes, "Brecht". To which the first character asks, "Then who is the play by?"

Of course plagiarism's a bad idea at any time and Brecht's case has never been as massively documented as it is here, so good on Fuegi, I guess, for blowing the whistle on him. I could wish, though, that the whistle-blower had brought a little more craft to his task, could write a cleaner page, than this one did or can. A sentence like "The important plays of the period are written only with Steffin's daily work" is just plain dopey, it's opaque or inept, in fact it's all of those things. It could imply a meaningful creative role for Steffin, or it could mean only that Steffin typed out Brecht's handwritten copy. There are so many equally sloppily-handled sentences here that finding and quoting them isn't even interesting, there's no triumph in it, it's shooting fish in a barrel. If there *is* any interest associated with it, it might come when you notice that the loosest writing of all coincides with the most blatant of the roundhouse swings, the blunderbuss barrages, that Fuegi lays on. It's as if his enthusiasm or fever-level picks up at these junctures and such little craft as he possesses gets left behind in the rising excitement altogether.

I would like at this point to do some leaving-behind of my own, and turn towards the Brecht I have one particularly private memory of. I remember one day a long while ago going into a theatre in Paris that was showing *Mère Courage* and then discovering (something I ought to have known before buying my ticket) that the company was Brecht's own, the Berliner Ensemble from East Germany, and that therefore the production was being given in German. Of which language I, at that time, did not understand a word.

This was depressing for about a quarter of an hour. In the next little while, though, without my asking myself why this was happening, the experience set about becoming as engrossing as anything—yes, *anything*—I'd ever known in a theatre; and it went on being so right up to the end of Act I. After the intermission all this repeated itself, the whole cycle: initial awareness, or remembering, that all this was in a language I had no access to, with its quite natural accompanying frustration; followed however within six or seven minutes by an immersion in the on-stage events that can be described in no milder way than *utter attention* (and a similarly 'utter' forgetting of any linguistic obstacle to my sharing in this experience). From then on the experience settled into being just plain marvelous until I was out in the Paris night again.

I've never forgotten that. What was going on on-stage, those archetypal movements of men and women and children, Mother Courage herself striding across Europe as the stage revolved through country after country—well, sophisticated dialogue was *not* what this was about; and although I'd never have guessed that anything this basic and primary-coloured would work *with* me or *on* me, work with and on me it did, and powerfully, movingly, and as you see, lastingly.

In other words the fact that I didn't understand a word of German didn't matter. Watching that stage, I *forgot* that I didn't understand the language that was being spoken. And this, although as a personal admission or claim it's of no interest, seems to me to matter here, where the context is a review of a book that invites us to be repelled to learn that others, not Brecht, are the real authors of these plays; a book that bases this charge at least to some degree on the unarguable fact that Brecht was no linguist and that his co-authors *were* accomplished linguists, fluent in French, English, etc; and that it is from works written in these other languages that much of the borrowings certainly come.

It matters, I think, because it may be that language never was nearly as central to the very great success of these plays as other components always were, components that Brecht may have been a near-genius in making use of; components such as, for instance, music; and, for another instance, a nearly unique sense of how certain basic human rhythms and rites (copulation, grief) can be invoked and presented on a stage and can then move an audience at a level beyond that which was, apparently, achievable by anybody else in this playwright's lifetime.

There are about two pages in Fuegi's book that acknowledge this level of emotional charge in Brecht's theatre, pages in which Fuegi quotes Eric Bentley and George Steiner and others as testifying to the almost unique power of the closing scene in one of the plays. Even here, however, it's as though he can't resist casting a negative light on it, which he does or tries to do by pointing out that emotional involvement of this sort runs counter to Brecht's celebrated 'Verfremdung' (alienation) theory—i.e. the theory that the task of the socialist playwright is to educate and enlighten his audience, and that therefore he ought not to issue that audience invitations to be 'carried away' emotionally, he should try to ensure that their critical and rational faculties are at all times intact. And at this point Fuegi has Brecht "grudgingly" confess that this is so.

Which should be enough, really, enough of a verbal mugging to satisfy anybody, but as it turns out is still not quite satisfying enough. Not for our devoted biographer and founder of the International Brecht Society. While he's about it, now that Verfremdung is on his mind, Fuegi cannot forbear to let us into one last secret. Brecht didn't, it seems, invent Verfremdung after all, not even the modern-day version of it. No, the true trail-blazer, Fuegi confides, was really the Soviet director Vesevolod Meyerhold, who had been "advocating (it) for two decades". So take, finally, that, BB.

E.E.Cummings

E.E.Cummings, A Biography by Christopher Sawyer-Laucanno

Odd to find the name capitalized in this book's title, 'e.e.cummings' being the enabling progenitor of a million lower-case poems, but his biographer tells us that at most other times—times outside poems—this is how his subject styled himself. That insistent lower-case usage (all those little i's instead of big I's in the poems) probably cost him a lot of mainline readers, but when you think about it, what's so special? The French 'je', German 'ich', Swedish 'jag', Italian 'io'…are we the only language-group to consider the first person singular so uniquely and erectly visible in the word-landscape?

Just a thought. There's a number of languages I'm not familiar with.

This is a longish, well-managed book (it's the most recent of three Cummings biographies) about a poet who probably reached more of that massive group of non-poetry-readers than just about anybody since the time of the Great Divide: since, I mean, the arrival of what's called Modernism, Eliot and Pound and the rout that followed them. Cummings, born in 1894, was a contemporary of both those poets but he wasn't all that impressed by either. He admired Pound up to a point, but had little tolerance for Eliot: this is just one of several things I like about him, there are more to come.

For one, it may well be (hard to be sure, it's so long ago) that the following EE poem, quoted here in full, was the poem that first jarred me loose from that 'massive' group I mentioned a minute ago. It's a lovely thing about William F. 'Buffalo Bill' Cody:

> Buffalo Bill's
> defunct
> who used to
> ride a watersmooth-silver

stallion
and break onetwothreefourfive pigeonsjustlikethat
                    Jesus
he was a handsome man
                    and what I want to know is
how do you like your blueyed boy
Mister Death

Yes, it's lovely all right, and unfollowable, if you try imitating it the odds are, well, they're impressive, that you're going to fail. You can't manoeuvre on a surface like that unless you're the man himself. And there are numbers of other poems nearly as fine. The trouble was, though, as people kept telling him, he frequently allowed this watersmooth-silvery surface of a poem to wander off into self-indulgence, and pretty often, too, he seemed to go out of his way to offend, to show his contempt for those folks whose inner lives were so boring, he felt, by contrast with his own—his own and the women he lived with and sometimes loved. (That's a topic, a field, I could use up my entire word-quota on, but will not, will just point you towards it: I think that this poet was a man of his time, readily available to women in a way I don't judge him for, a woman-adorer-and-praiser, sometimes arrogant and selfish and condescending, making as many wrong choices as were offered him, and now and then getting it right. He had three major loves, and timed things so that one of them was still around when he died, aged 67, of a cerebral hemorrhage, after chopping and stacking a bunch of logs outside his New Hampshire farmhouse).

He could also be, um, unsubtle. In this regard Sawyer-Maucanno (who has another and very different sort of literary biography on his cv., a biography of a writer who doesn't make either my short or long list, Paul Bowles) could be a lot harder on him than he is, and his book would be the better for it, the colder and clearer for it, but I don't want to push that too far—S-M likes Cummings a lot and since I also like him a lot, no push. Sometimes it seems merely adolescent crudeness, Cummings's unsubtlety; other times it adds up to a redeeming freshness, an airy and unforced newness. Here are the last two lines of a short poem explaining why he's so pleased to have come across Elaine, the first of the three major ladies mentioned above.

>   and possibly I like the thrill
>   of under me you so quite new

If you try reorganizing those thirteen words in the hope of improving things, marching them across their two lines in a more familiar pattern, you'll notice that they all go very quickly flat. Cummings relied on this sort of manual dexterity, he had a genius for it. In this case I imagine him starting off with a familiar thought couched in familiar words, and then lifting this or that word out of its place, unobtrusively slipping it back in further along, shifting that other one under it, eliminating those two or three altogether... *Elaine, Elaine, come look at this!*

Another morning with a special small joy in it for both of them, maybe.

I could go on for a long while with Cummings, with cummings also if that looks more familiar. There is what's probably his most-quoted poem, beginning "anyone lived in a pretty how town". There's the poem-as-picture ('concrete' poetry), one of which middle-period poems ends with "dragging the sea for dream –S", and that final big 'S' is out on its own at the bottom of the poem, an elongated 'S', a hook for that sea-dragging. Many more poems in that vein, some witty, some obvious, mere party-games at times. There's a prose book called *The Enormous Room*, based on a brief and unserious military imprisonment in Paris during World War One, where Cummings, aged 23, drove an ambulance for a bit, but mostly enjoyed Paris, its galleries, its streets, its bistros, and its 'putes', one of which latter group almost but not quite cost him his virginity (different strokes in those days, or fewer). He painted and sketched, not too interestingly if you ask me (if you ask S-M, the paintings are just as "new" as the poems, not derivative at all, he says; I find them derivative, very Wyndham Lewis-ish, kind of cubist too, hard not to be at that time). He had wonderful parents, a father in particular whose selfless and patient love for him rivals John Ruskin's father's devotion to *his* son; very moving it is, reading of fathers and sons like these, proof that the world knows secrets it seldom speaks of. Cummings, wonderful to relate, knew how to value this: "I was welcomed as no son of any king or queen was ever welcomed. Here was my joyous fate and my supreme future."

I'm happy to leave him so.

Frost

Robert Frost: A Life by Jay Parini

YESTERDAY WOULD HAVE been Frost's 125th birthday. He hasn't been around for the last 37 of those years but his biographers have stayed on the job uninterruptedly, so that the image, that tousle-headed, sturdy, not-so-old-looking man, has not faded, and the road he didn't take, the woods he stopped by, and the wall he mended are all very much part of what we know about him, and about America and its poetry.

Frost would probably feel all right that this is so. He certainly wanted his fame. What he wouldn't have been so keen about, surely, is the in-fighting of those biographers, scarcely one of whom has had a decent word to say about any of the others. Only three years ago I was reading a new-minted book with a remarkably similar title to this one (actually, it was called *Robert Frost*, period), a book which in spite of some weird interpretations of poems, had its points: notably, it told the reader a great deal more about the blighted lives of the Frost children than this book does.

It's a subject I find interesting. Genius in its effect on its children— overwhelmingly malign, I think. A little research into the lives of Thomas Mann, James Joyce, Victor Hugo, and many, many more, brings up a litany of suicides, asylums, and flights into mediocrity. The subject is as old as art itself, and is so richly complex as to merit a study by a more committed and generous talent than has, so far as I know, ever looked into it. But if Jay Parini, who has novels and poetry as well as a Steinbeck biography on his *résumé*, has less time for the children and their unlit lives than his predecessor, Jeffrey Meyers, had, he more than compensates elsewhere.

This newest arrival on the Frost shelf, written in a measured prose, keeps the central focus on the life, but also, as the years pass and the poetry begins to move and lift with that slow and eventually unmistakable Frostian ground-music, brings a confident and quite often fresh, quite often insightful eye to individual lyrics and lines. For some readers it may be this—these ascents, as they may feel, out of the Life into the Work—which will decide whatever rivalry there is among Frost's chroniclers. For others, and right now for this review, the life goes on.

Frost had a not untalented father who drank and who died young, and a Swedenborgian mother who held things together and who also, important to add, read imaginative (and not necessarily mainstream) stories, e.g. *At the Back of the North Wind,* to her children every night. There was never enough money on those farms in Massachusetts and New Hampshire where Robert was growing up, but a paternal grandfather seems to have listened when the boy's cries were loudest. Not unlike a few other men who ended up as mere 'writers', Frost initially wanted to be a professional athlete—but where playing goalkeeper for his nation's/university's football team was Camus's aim, also Nabokov's, also Rilke's (just kidding about that last one), Frost wanted to pitch in a World Series.

Needless to say, all of these early-days ambitions came to naught.

What Frost did at least begin to do, though, at the age of 15 and with the encouragement of a girl named Elinor in the same school-class, was write verse.

It is impractical, I think, to attempt to follow through the next decades in any detail. The detail is in Parini's book (the best of a restive bunch), in Meyers's book, and in a three-volume work by Lawrance Thompson which all other Frost-chroniclers unite in reviling (Thompson has been so enthusiastically hammered by every Frostian alive that I am sure, although I have made no enquiries in the matter, that he and his works must lie on that great remainder-table in the sky whence no riposte can ever come. I am sure of this because I think nobody would dare speak of the undead as his competitors have spoken of Lawrance Thompson.)

Enough to say that Frost married Elinor, that the two lived together until her death 63 years later, that the marriage looks on the page as though it had been scripted by Frost's contemporary Eugene O'Neill (i.e. broody and chill and grudging), that of their six children (see above, "children of genius", for a thumbnail glimpse of their lives) only one outlived Robert; that after Elinor's death there was an affair with a colleague's wife which drove Frost, in his own word, "crazy" for months; that during the last decades of his life he was fêted wherever he went, offered the least-demanding writer-in-residence postings ever—which is, trust me, saying something—won more Pulitzer Prizes (four) than anybody else ever has, famously read that poem at John F. Kennedy's inauguration, and died in 1963, full, truly, of years and honours.

Two further matters to mention. One is, as Parini reminds us, the role that England—not just its poetry, but the country itself—played in Frost's life as well as his art. Frost got a little money in 1912 and took his family across the sea and into the English countryside. He stayed there until late 1914, loving, it seems, every minute, and sailing home only when the money ran out and the menace of German subs was growing. What happened during those two English years was life-altering. Frost sought out poets in London, found some (Pound and T.E. Hulme right away; within a year he was dining alone with Yeats), and had his first two books published and praised by the leading reviewers in the land.

All this reads like a dream. By the time he was back in the U.S. the dream had crossed the sea ahead of him and had been seen and absorbed by the New York and Boston critics and publishers, so hard to impress before. If it were not, on a literal level, so obviously the reverse of true (he never ceased to be grateful for his experiences and his treatment in the U.K.), one could say that Frost never looked back.

England did one more thing for him which he never forgot. Off there in the Gloucestershire countryside Frost found "the best friend I ever had". This was Edward Thomas, whose poems about the fields and villages of England lying fallow and quiet because of the million dead in France, "whose feet, returning, lightly dance" might not have been written were it not for Frost's loving encouragement. Thomas had not realized, Frost said later, that his pages of prose were unwitting poetry, until he, Frost, pointed this out. Thomas's death at Arras two years after Frost had gone home was a blow of which Frost spoke often over the next half-century.

Parini does well to reminds us of all this. What he also does well, as I have suggested, is the intermittent work on The Work, of which I have said little. Rightly or wrongly, it's my guess that those who take the trouble to read this review know Frost's work well enough that they don't need me to hold forth on it. And I would only end up lulling you with old lines I still like a lot, the little horse, the snowy woods, and "the sweep/ Of easy wind and downy flake".

Flaubert

Flaubert, A Life by Geoffrey Wall

I'VE BEEN WAITING for this book for a long time. As a literary-biography junkie and confirmed admirer of Gustave Flaubert's *Un Coeur Simple, Bouvard et Pécuchet* and *Madame Bovary,* also one who thinks Flaubert's letters are the finest writer's-letters ever, it has been a source of major frustration, a pain in the everypart, really, that a first-rate biography of this man has not existed. And it hasn't. I've kept an eye out.

So it's a good feeling to be able to report that this most glaring of omissions in the genre is now, with the book presently under review, remedied. Frustrations over, pains fled. I couldn't be more grateful to the author of any book published this year than I am to Geoffrey Wall.

Wall, who teaches French at the University of York in the U.K., has achieved this with a book which although it is continuously vivid and lively, never falls into the trap that other biographers whose styles or ambitions might be felt to be similar ('vivid' etc) often do fall into: namely, telescoping complex and subtle aspects of their subject's life into slick generalizations which the reader is bound, before long, to recognize for what they are. Notable in this regard is Wall's use of the familiar but risky formula whereby the biographer, who often cannot track down a contemporary account to document what he or she right now wants to show, will begin a paragraph with "We may well suppose that...", or "Let us, then, picture him as he..."—a formula which is very likely to be fatal to the reader's trust that what he's reading is indeed a record of a lived life and not cross-dressed fiction.

It's instructive to find this biographer not only using the formula, but proving that in the right hands it can not only light up what might have been a pedestrian page, but that it can manage this without involving the reader in so much as a raised eyebrow.

Example. "We can be sure that Louis-Philippe's sudden elevation to the throne was the subject of animated conversation around the large, highly polished liberal dinner table of Dr.Achille-Cléophas Flaubert. The mood of the hour was generously optimistic…"

The "highly polished table" isn't one of the book's star pieces of furniture, this is its only moment and it's not a big one, but a glimpse of it leads the reader genially into that optimistic hour and the *cercle* of intimates of Gustave's father, and contributes, I think, its modest portion of glow to the picture of Rouen and Gustave's adolescence which follows.

Vivid life, in fact, is what this book richly provides its readers. Once one has got past the standard image of the uniquely dedicated artist, it's that vividness, that extra-human energy of the man, that sweeps all before it. Flaubert has been called, of course, a *monstre sacré*, the writer who stands out above all other writers (enormous claim!) as representing an unrelenting commitment to an ideal, to the 'exactly-right word' (*mot juste*), to an incessant reworking of the page before him. All true enough.

But the life! The energy smokes out of him, this very large green-eyed man, it enchants Turgenev and George Sand life-long and many others too, and as for what it does inside the covers of his best books—! I could fill every bit of space left to me with quotations that cut to the chase so brusquely as to rattle your teeth. And now that that's been thought of, why not?

Already as an adolescent, surveying his probable future among the comfortable citizens of Rouen, and not liking what he saw, he writes, not unbluntly, "Am I to live like a king, or a pig?"

And much later and quite a lot more subtly, there's this passage, which offers not only a quick sketch of Emma Bovary's lover, Léon (after he has turned away from Emma and from passion and settled down) but also a well-aimed and, at the end, lyrical shot at Flaubert's favourite target: "He gave up the flute, the exalted feelings, the imagination. For every bourgeois, in the heat of youth, if only for a day, has believed himself capable of immense passions, of heroic deeds; every solicitor carries inside him the ruins of a poet."

Not unrelated to that, there's *this*, explaining why he spent four entire years writing *Madame Bovary*, why he dedicated all those mornings and late afternoons to the deliberate, unhurried depiction of a class of humanity he despised (this writer who more than any other *nailed* the word '*bourgeoisie*', gave it all the smug, hypocritical, unadventurous connotations it has never, since then, managed to shake free from): "I abhor ordinary existence. Personally, I have always held myself as aloof from it as I could. But aesthetically I wanted this once—and only this once—to plumb its depths."

In this regard *Madame Bovary* ends with what I believe to be the single most crushing final sentence of any novel I know. The "He" in the sentence is one Homais, a pharmacist in the provincial town which has been the scene of the naïve and pitiable lives and deaths of Charles and Emma Bovary. More than anyone else in the novel, as his early servilities and deceits and hypocrisies lead him, apparently inevitably, towards his eventual status as the bullying and pompous conscience of the town, Homais personifies that 'ordinary existence' Flaubert so 'abhorred'; he is spread out in all his contemptible detail for us, impaled, it's not too much to say, for our unhurried study and attention. The final sentence, set out in a paragraph all its own, is: "*Il vient de reçevoir la croix d'honneur*".*

Here is Flaubert's celebrated explanation of the *sheer private joy* of writing, a passage in which he's explaining his own intimate participation in the emotions and sights and sounds of Emma's ride through the forest with her second lover, Rodolphe. "…it is a delicious thing to write, whether well or badly—to be no longer yourself but to move in an entire universe of your own creating. Today, for instance, man and woman, lover and beloved, I rode in a forest on an autumn afternoon under the yellow leaves, and I was also the horse, the leaves, the wind, the words my people spoke, even the red sun that made them half-shut their love-drowned eyes….Praised be the Lord for not creating me a cotton merchant, a vaudevillian, a wit, etc.!"

And in the novel we can find what he did, a few sentences of it, with that "entire universe" during that particular day's session at his desk. "…the horizontal sun passing between the branches dazzled the eyes. Here and there around her, in the leaves or on the ground,

---

*"He has just been given the Cross of the Legion of Honour." (Trans. Paul de Man)

trembled luminous patches, as if humming-birds flying about had scattered their feathers. Silence was everywhere; something sweet seemed to come forth from the trees. She felt her heartbeat return, and the blood coursing through her flesh like a river of milk. Then far away, beyond the wood, on the other hills, she heard a vague prolonged cry, a voice which lingered, and in silence she heard it mingling like music with the last pulsation of her throbbing nerves."

The passage comes back to earth and to a hint of what's ahead in its last sentence. "Rodolphe, a cigar between his lips, was mending with his penknife one of the two broken bridles."

In a letter, "You can portray wine, love, women, glory, on condition of being neither a drinker, a lover, a husband, or a soldier. Immersed in life, you canot see it clearly…an artist is a monstrosity, a thing outside nature".

And, "May I die like a dog rather than try to rush through even one sentence before it is ripe."

And, "The morality of art consists in its beauty, and I value style even more than truth."

And, "Of all lies, art is the least untrue".

And another line to be taken to heart: "Honours dishonour, titles degrade…" True, all true, whatever ambivalent echoes it has. Equally helpful to meditate upon when the honours and titles do *not* arrive as when they *do*. (The sentence, to be honest here, is triadic and ends with "employment stupefies",which although surely often true, we may, when we remember his mother's house and money, his freedom to take those long and solitary pipe-smoking strolls by the river in the grounds of Le Croisset every late afternoon prior to joining her at the dinner-table, consider to be just fine for Gustave but less helpful to *hoi polloi* like us.)

He was a splendidly inventive scatologist and a trustworthy friend. Both are shown in the letters to Alfred LePoittevin, later to Maxim DuCamp, with whom he journeyed unhurriedly in the Near East, tasting and later recalling its pleasures. There are the forthright, often scornful, often ribald letters to his longterm mistress Louise Colet, who, off there in Paris and forbidden to show her face in Rouen, took it all and kept coming back—or rather, kept staying there—for more.

And there is that very close relationship with his mother, who was aware of her son's gifts but took care not to flatter him unduly. He reported in a letter that she once said to him, "Your mania for sentences has dried up your heart". His comment on this? "Sublime".

And so it is. And so, just about, is this book.

Céline

Céline: A Biography by Frederic Vitoux

THE LIST OF ENTRE-DEUX-GUERRES French novelists who contributed
to the anti-Semitic clamour on which the Nazis gratefully built is not
just long, it's almost all-inclusive. Easier by far to mention those who
steered clear of that *dreck* than those who willingly waded in. Really,
you have to wait until the Liberation and the appearance of soon-
familiar names like Camus, Sartre and de Beauvoir before the taking
of a deep freshsmelling breath at any Paris literary gathering begins
to seem a good idea (and even those three might be, in any really
radical, really taking-a-risk sense, two too many; safest to stick to a
tête-à-tête with Camus). Gide, Valéry, Bernanos, Claudel, Daudet,
Giraudoux—that list could be tripled and there'd still be a few left
stuffing their peculiar hooked-cross regalia and undesirable letter-
heads into the stove in the back room of the *maison de campagne*.
Academicians and Goncourt winners and even a *Nobeliste* is there,
all of them eminent and gifted and praised and none of them, in this
regard, much help when what you want is a corner of the Reading
Room your soul can feel comfortable in.

Among all these, Louis-Ferdinand Céline is a tarnished star.
Hugely more gifted than most of them, a writer whose effect on his
native language has many times been compared to Joyce's effect on
English, at the age of 40 (having published two brilliant books) he
falls off his apparently guaranteed perch among the *immortels* and
straight down into one of the deepest and darkest circles of hell, a
Jew-baiter-and-harrier noticeable for his vindictiveness even among
all those others. *Why* he did this is a question his biographer has no
interesting answer to. Perhaps there is no interesting answer, only, as
Hannah Arendt says elsewhere, banal answers. A father who muttered
unpleasantnesses into a child's ear, a job he didn't get, a woman he
lost to a man who might have been a Jew? Or none of the above,

something else equally out-of-scale.

Enough to say that in 1932, aged 38, Céline published his most-famous-by-far novel *Journey to the End of Night*, more resonantly *Voyage au Bout de la Nuit*. It's a novel which in the puddles at its bottom end can sound like one of Henry Miller's *Tropics* (listen to this: his narrator's just arrived in New York and the women impress him: "These apparitions seemed all the more divine to me as they appeared totally unaware of my existence on the next bench, all senile and drooling with erotico-mystical admiration, quinine, and, I must admit, hunger as well. They could take me away, sublimate me, those unbelievable shopgirls, all they had to do was make one move, but I guess they had other things to do....". Well, no, it's not quite Miller, is it. Miller's shopgirls would have been all over him, in seconds and for hours. Still, the erotico-mystical business sounds pretty familiar.) Quite a lot further up the scale, though, this *Journey* is, even in translation, reminiscent of, yes, *Ulysses*. And Céline followed it with *Death on the Instalment Plan*, a cracklingly energetic text which has, like *Journey*, not a single Jewish character in it. (This is good? Well, Frederic Vitoux thinks it is, and, in the context of what will follow, yes, it's good.)

Of these early-and-middle-period books Vitoux writes, in one of the very few passages worth quoting from this biography, "There is the velocity of language, of course. He is the man who bevels sentences, disarticulates syntax, who warps and straightens words so as to hurl them at great speed towards emotion, the ultimate target". Well said, what a fine description of a marvellous sort of writing! (Some might argue with that designation of the "ultimate target", but not me.)

And then it all falls down. In 1937 Céline writes *Bagatelle for a Massacre* and in the next year he writes *The School of Corpses*. Both these fester with his contempt for the "spineless" Republic he has come to associate with its Jewish Prime Minister, Leon Blum, with Jewish money, Jewish-dominated literary juries, with the whole hallucinatory landscape he has strayed into by this time. His letters, too, show the extent of his obsession. He publishes articles, essays, editorials, all on the same theme. It's a personal crusade by now, it seems to owe as good as nothing even to the propaganda outpourings from Nazi

Germany: so it would seem, anyway , judging from his comment that "to chose between the Germans and the Reds is like choosing between cholera and the plague". (Incidentally, we're out of luck here too: "Canada, the most damned boring country there is…")

Until at the end, at war's near-end, when all his coevals have scuttled for cover and somehow found it, Céline's high and dry and exposed in all his naked hysteria, fleeing with his last duchess via a jigsaw of unlit trains across burning Germany to Denmark, where, celebrated as he is, he's interned and then is allowed to stay in exile until an amnesty in 1952 brings him back to France and one last big book, *North*, published a year before his death in 1960. It's a mostly bleak, occasionally lyrical story set in northern Europe, on the plains of Brandenburg and in the wildernesses even further East, a place that seems part-Russia part-Apocalypse, a continent-size canvas which reminds me, at times very strikingly, of Michel Tournier's *The Erl-King*. I prefer that book to anything Céline ever wrote but it occurs to me that it may owe quite a lot to the uneasy genius of Tournier's erratic predecessor.

Borges

Doctor Brodie's Report by Jorge Luis Borges

"I HAVE DONE MY BEST—I don't know with what success—to write straightforward stories. I do not dare state that they are simple; there isn't anywhere on earth a single page or single word that is, since each thing implies the universe, whose most obvious trait is complexity..."

Those lines, from a preface Borges wrote for the volume of short stories entitled *Doctor Brodie's Report*, represent their author with what is, I think, a splendid and misleading clarity. On the one hand lucid and accurate; on the other artifice-laden and profound, and releasing, when even the slightest of mind-pressure is applied to them, unemphatic wisdom of an order seldom audible in these swollen times. Comparing Borges to even your (or my) respected novelists of this new century in terms of subtlety or refinement of sensibility is like comparing the often-invoked lost library of Alexandria to the building on the east side of Yonge just north of Bloor: there is much to be learned from the latter, but one's deepest nostalgia (even though we'll never find the stack-pass to let us in) is for the former.

The analogy's strained, Borges is no burnt-out case, his work's accessible and vital. Somehow, though, due maybe to the combination of his final-years' blindness* with the sparingly-issued pages (such quality on so few pages that one tends to read them as last whispers from a vanished super-culture), I don't find the analogy overdone. Reading this man you're jarred into remembering what words can do, how precisely they can point and how endlessly evoke. Each word's an iceberg-tip, I could say, except that no, that's not a humanly-inhabited image, and Borges's art is full of centuries of humanity, speaking usually in an admirably unapocalyptic voice

—————
*When he was read aloud to, day after day for months, by the very young Alberto Manguel.

95

Elusive, too, that voice. At times its links with normally-recognized experience are so threadlike you bend to listen. One of my most frequently self-administered wisdom-bits is not from Borges but Stendhal: "We must write as though for a generation infinitely more subtle than our own." Borges went a step further: he *became* that generation. In his writings he quite often turns back and gestures at us, slight movements we can honour ourselves by trying to understand.

As for his own attitude to all this, it is not omniscient, indeed at times he seems as puzzled as we are. Here are two comments, again from the preface to these stories: "The art of writing is mysterious; the opinions we hold are ephemeral, and I prefer the Platonic idea of the Muse to that of Poe, who reasoned, or feigned to reason, that the writing of a poem is an act of the intelligence." And, "After all, writing is nothing more than a guided dream."

Most of the stories in *Doctor Brodie's Report* are given to us at second-or-third hand. Some are gaucho-legends told to the narrator in waterfront Buenos Aires bars, some are speculations on events which possibly were never enacted but which later on, in the imagination, grew uncontrollably; it's as if they had been so powerfully dwelt on in the mind that life now can neither suppress nor slow them. I hope that you may, in the following passage, sense the distinctive quality of this Argentinian writer's voice, the words coming off the page like the unstressed sounds from a palimpsested tablet which knows very well what's on the mostly-obliterated layers beneath but declines, out of pride, out of the absolute conviction of its rank, of what it owes to its family's long dialogues with itself, to tell us about it. The passage is from a story called *The Elder Lady*.

"Mrs. Jauregui never went out of the house after 1921; perhaps she never suspected that Buenos Aires had been changing and growing. First memories are the most vivid. The city that she pictured beyond her front door may well have been a much earlier one than that of the time they were forced to move from the center of town out to Palermo. If so, to her the oxen that hauled wagons still rested in the square of the Once, and dead violets still spread their fragrance among the gardens of Barracas. 'Now all my dreams are of dead people', was one of the last things she was heard to say. No one had ever thought of her as a fool, but as far as I know she had never enjoyed the pleasures of the mind; the last pleasures left her would be those of memory and, later on, of forgetfulness. She had always beeen generous. I recall her bright, quiet eyes and her smile. Who knows what tumult of passions—now lost but which once burned—there had been in that old woman; in her day, she had been quite pleasant-looking. Sensitive to plants, whose modest and silent life was so akin to her own, she looked after some begonias in her room and touched their leaves, which she could no longer see. Up until 1929, the year in which she sank into a kind of half-sleep, she recounted historical happenings, but always using the same words in the same order, as if they were the Lord's Prayer, so that I grew to suspect there were no longer any real images behind them. Even eating one thing or another was all the same to her. She was, in short, happy."

Graves

Robert Graves: Life on the Edge by Miranda Seymour

ONCE IN SWEDEN somebody told me, to my undisguised incredulity, that he had called upon Robert Graves at his house in Majorca and, the poet being away, had been given permission to spend the night in a garden shed on the property. Months later, he said, the shed was still his home and Graves still unglimpsed. Having now read Miranda Seymour's fine biography, it seems not too soon to acknowledge that that story just might have been true. The images it suggests, so generous, so careless, so ramshackle, are borne out in every chapter here.

Robert Graves had a long life: 1895-1985. It is fair to say, too, that he was seldom idle. Fifty-five collections of poetry, fifteen novels, ten translations, an autobiography that is still the bestselling memoir in English of life in World War One's trenches, forty works of non-fiction, one biography (of T.E.Lawrence). His book on the myth-centred sources of poetry, *The White Goddess*, was called "the chief holy book of my poetic conscience", by Ted Hughes. I liked it for a while too. It has provided metaphors and symbols for, modestly estimated, a half-million poems, not all of them bad. In spite of all this, international fame and affluence kept on not quite arriving until his latter years, when television touched him with its cure-all wand. *I Claudius* and *Claudius the King* are familiar titles.

Something else about this English writer is of interest. It is his devotion to 'the Muse': the pattern which shows poetic creation as endlessly ignited by women. Graves was typical of his generation and his nationality in that he came late and uninformed to women; public school did that to its clients, and did other things too. Seymour writes of her subject when he is 22: "He must have been aware by now that almost every man with whom he had a close friendship was homosexual". Among the close friends were Siegfried Sassoon, the 'Georgian poetry' anthologist Edward Marsh, Lytton Strachey and Peter Johnstone, the last-named a school-companion who very probably appears, Seymour suggests, as "Marjorie" in the above-mentioned war memoir, *Goodbye To All That*.

This awareness on Graves's part may, the reader is led to feel, have a direct connection with his early marriage to Nancy Nicholson, who was 19, artistic (she illustrated a number of children's books), independent, and at the time of their engagement was doing war work as a labourer and wearing "mannish breeches".

Casting breeches to one side, it should also be said that Nancy and Robert had four children, that Robert wrote to her "every day" during any early-year absences, that he made a lot of poems and she did a lot of print-making; in short, that if all was not well, neither, for a time, was all ill. Nevertheless the usual problems accompanying writers' marriages (that engrossed solitary activity) were apparently exacerbated by an extreme inflexibility, or, if you prefer, absolute sense of integrity, on Nancy's part. Two examples: she once returned a painting given by her brother, the artist Ben Nicholson, because it contained, she said, "a displeasing colour"; and, writes Seymour, "she would walk out of a room if a guest wore a colour that clashed with it".

Nothing of this might have been a problem if Laura Riding had not appeared. One of the most welcome feats of Seymour's book is to bring clarity to this mysterious figure: a 24-year-old American who had written, to all intents and purposes, one poem, a poem which had won a prize Stateside and which Graves had admired and had written its author to say so—and who, largely on the strength of this letter, showed up on the Graves's doorstep and didn't go away for fifteen years. She epitomized in her small self quite a few of the aspects of the 'white goddess', that metamorphosing embodiment of Woman (Mother, Lover, Witch) from one phase of whom Graves would, as Riding began helping him to understand, receive as a gift all of his poetry-to-come. He also began to understand that not only Nancy but also his children, his mother, and his friends, would from now on be effectively banished.

It's a long and, yes, fascinating story, and one which I'd rather not misrepresent by shortcutting where I shouldn't. Sufficient, though, perhaps, to say that Riding's arrival launched Graves toward the view that would sustain him for another 40-years'-worth of poems, and that would justify, in his eyes and the eyes of a few others too, the adopting, the commandeering almost, of a series of 'Muses'—young women who would, in theory, position themselves just out of carnal reach but near enough for the poet to stretch towards them with his Myth-driven words. And so, for the next 40 years, it was. In her turn the quite-bright but egregious Laura Riding eventually sidles offscreen to be replaced by Juli, Cindy Lee, Margot and a few even more ephemeral others; not all of them alike, need it be said, but all filling the same role and, here's the interesting part, all confidently defined by the ageing Graves in that same way—as the Court of Love's unattainable beloved, the troubadour's Lady of the Castle, the beckoning Eros in the form of a woman. Graves had already inscribed this as a form of poetic canon in *The White Goddess*, perhaps without knowing the extent to which he would embody it (with the apparent approval of Beryl, his second wife) for the rest of his life.

The obvious, so far unraised question is, how well did he practice it? Or, same thing, how meaningfully, how obediently did the myth serve him? And that's a question Graves doesn't get to decide, his readers do. Ninety percent of his poetry is, Seymour has counted it all up, love poetry. Seymour rightly describes this as "romantic, moon-haunted"; in the same paragraph she goes on to say, but wrongly now, I think, that it's "beyond reproach". Hardly any poems truly deserve such an extreme comment, Keats's *Odes* certainly, here and there single poems by Hardy or Herbert or Gray or Frost or Edward Thomas or Larkin, several by Yeats—none by Robert Graves. Graves over-wrote at all times, every poem, and he went on writing and publishing too long, into senile embarrassment. But there are some lovely lyrics which almost anyone would be happy to have in his 'collected' (it has to be a 'his', the pronouns inside the poem would make that clear), and as for the life, Miranda Seymour's really rather brilliant book shows an untidy and at times foolish man whose energies and joys and griefs nevertheless continually, on page after page, lift the spirit, lift it either a little or more than that. At the risk of making it into the blurbs on the back cover of any further editions of this book, I think it may be the literary biography of the year.

Camus

Albert Camus: A Life by Olivier Todd

IS THERE ANY WRITER alive today with half the dazzle that Albert Camus had for almost a generation following upon the end of the Second World War? He had so much going for him!—the connection with the Resistance, his columns in *Combat*, the instant postwar availability of *L'Étranger* (its stripped-down vocabulary repelled the bourgeoisie almost as much as did its amorality, and these two qualities together made it a natural for the young), the suffering Sisyphus, the Notebooks, his dark good looks, it all added up to an oddly (no, not oddly, an understandably) noble aura that wouldn't go away. This in spite of his dubious on-and-off friends, Sartre and de Beauvoir and a lot of unknown-to-history people in black turtle-necks.

Hard to beat. There were then two more novels, several plays, and a number of much-discussed essays, one of which began with the provocative line, "There is only one serious philosophical problem, which is suicide". There were travels abroad and, at the young age of 43, a Nobel Prize. And death three years later in a car driven by his publisher's son.*

If the work's quality is truly special there is no reason why death should blur a writer's popularity, and it is good to learn from this biography that *L'Étranger* (variously translated as *The Outsider* and *The Stranger*), *The Plague* and *The Fall* are currently ranked in France as equal in public esteem to the works of just one other writer (that this 'one other writer' is Marcel Pagnol is disheartening, but *passons*). I wish that Olivier Todd had told us how long this has been the case.

---

*The Camus-myth didn't like this version of his death and substituted, for years, a version in which Camus was at the wheel and wanted to die, i.e., he had to be not just a great writer but also James Dean.

It's my feeling, based on much listening to university students, that the Sixties and Seventies had little use for Camus, with his credo of struggle, man-as-Sisyphus forever pushing that rock up that mountain and then *awarely* walking back down in order to start over again.** The slogans of the Sixties and early Seventies (preferable as some of them seem to me to have been to today's buzz-phrases) had more to say about going with the flow than they did about struggle.

Back from the theory to the life. Todd's book is the most detailed account to come along of the days and nights of this hugely admired man. Here the reader can learn of the many loves Camus had, a trite item in the histories of many artists but not so trite here, where there was a lot less deceit than is often the case, and of hypocrisy or posturing, practically nothing at all. This does not exactly merit bouquets, since there was a wife and children, but it's something. Women liked him quickly and didn't stop liking him when he left. In fact, you could almost say that he never 'left' anybody, since letters came and went years after a parting, and rekindlings happened. This is not usual and not, surely, judgeable.

Interesting, too, to finally get some clarity regarding his wartime years. There was no, repeat no collaboration, instead there was a growing commitment to writing and editing the underground newspaper *Combat*. In that 'active' regard the record easily outshines, say, Sartre. Camus declined to have anything to do with those writers and publishers and entertainers who played it both ways, *collaborateur* today and *résistance* hero tomorrow, people like the dramatist Paul Claudel, the dancer Serge Lifar and the world-charmer Maurice Chevalier to name only a few of dozens.

Still, life for Albert was not half bad. Tuberculosis had kept him out of military service (as it had kept him from his dream-career, which was playing goal for the French national football team). This was good luck enough, one would think, without the additional bonus of spending the evening of D-Day, while the Normandy beaches were

---

**It was quite exactly that awareness—that there will be no revelation, no reward, no epiphany, no transfiguration to be expected or believed-in as resulting from this striving, but that it is nonetheless the striving that describes and defines mankind—that was, for Camus, the proof of humanity's unquenchable nobility.

still lit-up and lethal, at a party with the gifted and seriously-beautiful actress Maria Casarès, a party from which the two of them returned "by bicycle, a bit drunk, with Maria riding on the handlebars."

That's a picture I'm happy to add to my cache of Camus-images.

Speaking as one who has reread *L'Étranger* (and yes, I do mean *L'Étranger* and not either *The Outsider* or *The Stranger*) more often than any other book (it is very short) and who still admires this writer for the gravity and the purity of so many of his pages, it is comforting and not at all diminishing to meet him here in the years of his apprenticeship. André Malraux was an idol whose every suggestion, every tip, was reverently adopted. The killing-scene in *L'Étranger* was, Malraux commented, "good but not convincing", Camus would "have to try harder". And as if not trusting him to figure out what to do about this on his own, Malraux magisterially nudges him along: "One more paragraph, about the link between the sun and the Arab's knife...is needed". Heady stuff.

All in all, then, this is a comprehensively researched life. That it has no flow to it, that it reads woodenly, every second sentence coming onto the page as if it has not been introduced to anything nearby, is unfortunate but may be partly the translator's doing. The silly bits have to be Todd's alone: a line like "His heart and body required the right to unlimited love", is only the most majestic of many in this regard. Take what you can get, though. The detail is dense and largely new, and the accomplishment of the artist whose name is on the cover outshines all.

I'm so attached to this man's work and life, and I so unequivocally failed ever to meet him, that I must, compensatorily, append to this review the news that I was living in Stockholm when he arrived there to receive his Nobel. I was walking on the town's main street, Kungs-gatan, when the limo carrying the *Nobeliste* drove slowly past. People stopped and bowed, men doffed their hats. I was so moved by this that I failed to bow. Camus, sitting beside his wife, looked straight ahead, gloomily.

I tried putting 'despairingly' there, but it kept looking false. I'd have needed to be closer.

Orwell

Orwell: The Authorized Biography by Michael Sheldon

JUST TO SEE THE NAME on the cover is enough to start you thinking *this had better be good.* Because *who* (the name on the cover makes you think) among biographers could possibly have decided he or she was up to this job—up to this half-thousand-page encounter with this austere and ascetic and *überall* revered presence among 20th-century masters?

And yet Sheldon's book isn't, to be honest, bad—it's only (to continue being honest) bad at the beginning. There's a naïve intro-duction in which he explains why his book is so much superior to another Orwell biography I happen to have read, one by Bernard Crick (a book which I thought was OK although, yes, it trudges). And I do think Sheldon might have acknowledged, while telling us about this superiority of his, that he had the great good luck to be writing his version of the *Life* after Orwell's wife's death, which meant he had access to materials which that wife jealously or faithfully had kept from any and all prying eyes. From, all that matters here, Crick's eyes.

So, not a good start, but things improve. For one admirable thing, Sheldon never tries to upstage his subject. This is rarer than you might think, it might even be a matter worth going into at length sometime. Also, his research was obviously comprehensive, and although he clearly likes Orwell a lot he manages to write of him without exagger-ation or babble. I read his book with mounting trust and ended it with a much-enhanced understanding of and respect for his subject. At its most stripped-down, this may be all we are entitled to require of a biographer, and it may also be what, when we find it, we should straightforwardly praise.

But what I really need to say is that having finished reading this book I went back and re-read a book I last looked at 30 years ago, a book you'll probably have read too, one which, along with *Animal Farm,* is the reason Orwell rose out of his mostly-life-long anonymity and became what he became (see above, "revered", etc)—I'm referring to the book entitled *1984;* and I need to add that the net result of both of these reads is that I am bowled over by the sheer quality of Orwell's gift. If I ever knew, before, how good he was, what I knew must have faded; I'd pigeon-holed him as a pretty good politically-oriented writer of Spanish Civil War vintage, and that was about it. I'll suppose nothing would have led me to pick up any of his works again if it hadn't been for this most recent biography.

No, there's one more thing I knew about Orwell. I remembered that in an obscure book review which Crick, not Sheldon, quotes from, Orwell had written something I'd thought important. Any work of literature, he'd written, however imaginative and soaring, had better keep in at least minimal touch with this earth we live on or else it will ultimately not retain our interest. It will fade and fail. "The written word loses its power", he'd written (and I'd copied this down, because I didn't own the Crick) "if it departs too far…from the ordinary world where two and two make four". Over the years I'd checked this out a few times against specific and briefly popular works, and concluded that it was true. It was also, I knew, written entirely against the tide.

I'll admit to wishing Sheldon had mentioned this, had quoted this. I'll also admit to wondering whether, granted that he did not mention or quote it, there might be a lot of similar *aperçus* Sheldon had passed on. This particular quotation was only a quick paragraph in an obscure journal, but retrieving specially glinting things like this, little essences from large minds, may be what first-class biographical research is about.

Never mind. Orwell emerges from these 564 pages as one of the most decent, likeable men of his stature-in-the-arts I've ever encountered; only Chekhov and Kafka are up there beside him. He's so decent and so honest it makes you feel, as the celebrated poem has it, you must change your life. It also makes you feel you should get out of the light and let Orwell speak for himself.

Of his earliest, creaking novels: "One difficulty I have never solved is that one has masses of experience which one passionately wants to write about, and no way of using them except by disguising them as a novel."

The first sentence in a book review: "As Mr.Cyril Connolly is almost the only novel reviewer in England who does not make me sick, I opened this, his first novel, with a lively interest."

No one was better at calling spades shovels. He reminds me of Doris Lessing in his angry refusal to allow artists privileges beyond the norm: if he could assess the art, he must also, he held, be permitted to assess the man or the woman. "One ought to be able to hold in one's head simultaneously the two facts that Dali is a good draughtsman and a disgusting human being."

I'd forgotten, also, how subtly, even when he's in the midst of a primarily emotional passage, he writes. He just never gets a handle on allowing the insistent intelligence of his thought to be submerged or tempered by the awkward fact that he's feeling moved by his subject matter. Here is *1984's* Winston Smith remembering his mother, how she had held him close in their desperate poverty: "It would not have occurred to her that an action which is ineffectual thereby becomes meaningless."

"Good prose", he wrote near the end of his life, "is like a window pane." To read him is like entering a word-space of pure crystal. I know of no one who writes like this today.

Proust

Marcel Proust: A Life by William C. Carter

IN AN OFTEN SELF-INDULGENT book (called *Modern Epic*) that has, however, dozens of bright moments, Colombia University critic Franco Moretti answers the question of what the characteristics of a world text are: "That's easy. It's very long, and very boring".

Certainly Marcel Proust's *In Search of Lost Time* is, if anything is, a world text. And though few today argue with the judgment that it can colonize a reader's mind more completely than most art dreams of doing, it does not always evade Moretti's half-frivolous definition. Even when Proust's novel in its several instalments began to be published, during the second decade of the recently retired century, opinions varied. Most of the leading French writers had no doubt that this cathedral of a story was outside any recognized category, that it would become a classic in whatever 'category' it might establish—indeed, the generosity of the responses from many members of the Paris literary establishment is so extreme that it make you wonder if anything half as unselfish would have surfaced in any other of the world's capitals.

That said, however, critical voices *were* raised. "Far too long", said one of Proust's wisest counselors, Louis de Robert. De Robert admired the work greatly—it was not too long for *him*, he said, but he felt that the generality of readers would never tolerate such length, such detail. "Endless sentences that roam about aimlessly", a reviewer wrote. And another noted that 30 small-print pages detailing the stages in a young man's getting dressed in the morning might be a few more pages than the world really needed.

When all is said and done—a phrase, I'd better add, that is so much at odds with anything remotely Proustian that I hope I intend it as a leg-pull—the kind of thing Proust achieved in his 4000 pages of uniquely minute reminiscences, of intensively remembered childhood, of yearnings for his beloved mother, of personalized requiems over his dead or rejected friends, of agonizings over the ideal lover he never found and surely, himself, never was—this kind of thing in its sheer extent had never been offered to readers in any culture before and has not been glimpsed anywhere since.

All this from a delicate, usually sick, sexually disastrous, court-eous-beyond-reason man of unparalleled kindness. A man who wrote—I haven't counted them—thousands of paragraphs that reach an intricacy and an acuity almost new to literature, breathtaking, often, in the shadowless human depths they invite us to look into.

People have analyzed these paragraphs in many a critical text, sometimes brilliantly, sometimes not. Sometimes in great scything generalities, sometimes the microscopic reverse. A German critic goes both ways in one sentence: "Proust takes particular delight in depen-dent clauses, because they illustrate the dependence of man upon chance, of the individual upon the whole."

Which says something interesting about dependent clauses, and one's glad to learn it. But if I'm sure of anything, it is that the reason Proust took delight in those clauses was not because they illustrated what the German critic says they illustrated. Proust wrote as he did because he was in search of the frailest, most thread-like, most evanescent truth of this or that relationship or episode or experience—and he searched in words, in sentences, in paragraphs; this was how he made his unhurried way towards truth. This is why his sentences accumulated and diminished and rose again, and sank and rose and trailed apparently off only to return again, as if they had forgotten something and so were coming back for it, in the way that a mind in search of the finest possible gathering of the most transient emotions of an evening or a day or a year will do. Hence the dependent clauses. To picture Proust's delight as he notices how his dependent clauses have, *sacré bleu*, once again illustrated one or another abstract circum-stance…I don't think so.

William Carter teaches French at the University of Alabama, and has written a previous book on Proust, as well as co-producing an award-winning documentary on the author. His *Marcel Proust* is the first major new life in decades, the first serious competition for George Painter's *Marcel Proust* (two volumes, 1959 and 1965). If it is a competition, I think it's a stand-off. Painter's book is witty, economical, on a page-by-page basis incomparably better written and more discriminatingly managed. It's no wonder that for all these years nobody wanted to take it on, in spite of the temptations offered by its subject's always-rising star.

Carter represents a more recent but increasingly familiar type: the scholar who chooses his subject, establishes his credentials in unremarkable stages (articles, reviews, travel grants, fellowships, larger grants) and finally lands one of the really big purses and gives to his chosen subject ten years or more of his life. Or of her life. Without necessarily knowing how to write a half-decently-turned sentence. I don't think there's a memorable or a pleasingly quotable paragraph in these 900-plus pages.

On the other hand, Carter has a lot of information that Painter either did not have or chose not to use. On the "life" as opposed to the "art" front, Carter wins. The reader learns details of Proust's illnesses (asthma all his life; a sensibility so fragile you would not want to shake its hand for fear of its screams); details of his pitiable, repellent, then pitiable again, then even more repellent, sexuality; details of friendships, betrayals, the political climate of 1920s Europe, the fathomless trickiness of publishers. And one learns of an endearing naiveté that this man, who was one of Europe's all-time great sophisticates, retained from childhood to the end of his life. In a letter to a friend, written when he was in his forties, Proust explains the nature of his masterpiece: "I don't know whether I told you that this book is a novel. At least it's from the novel form that it departs least. There is a person who narrates and who says 'I'".

Literary Biographies

IT'S BEEN SUGGESTED TO ME that I spend a little time, a few pages, on literary biographies, always the bookshop-shelves I stand longest at. I could begin by claiming that this interest dates from that stage of my own life at which I had, as Mallarmé famously wrote, "*lu tous les livres*", i.e. read all the major poems, all the classic novels, the plays, and had therefore to find something else to do with my need to read. Not a great start, though, would you say? Not totally false, as things go, but…not really likeable. OK if one is Mallarmé, eyebrow-raising otherwise. So, trying again, I'll say that one of the ground-level explanations for this tried-and-true interest is the strength of my feelings for what is past. My love for gone things. For my own childhood, yes, for whatever out-of-focus images float near from that lost time; but more importantly—because the vista then becomes so much farther-horizoned, so limitless—for things *way* back, for people and scenes and words from long before I was around. Those 'lost childhood' images and cries exist in all of us, wanted or unwanted they will sometimes intervene when the time-of-day seems right to them, they need no invitation from us to do that. But the huge canvas of everything else, ah, that's different. And that's where, for me, histories and biographies come in. And among the latter, the biographies of writers. Writing is what I've been doing for a lot of my longish life, so it makes sense that it should be the lives of writers I feel closest to. The lives of certain chosen ones among them, that is. Writers whom I arrived too late to know personally but whose books (novel after novel, poem after poem, play after play) may continue, as I go on reading them and as my trust in their author gathers and builds and becomes, finally, secure, to provide a voice filled with that very special 'seriousness' that the poet Philip Larkin has movingly told us we all, or a great many of us, quietly yearn for. To me it seems the most natural thing in the world to wish to know what may, what *can* be known of the lives and minds that shaped the particular sentences, pages, books, that have become such close companions in my life.

I'm not even remotely talking about what was called, in a journalistic piece I read not long ago, "the heuristic poverty of biographical explanations of works of art". I don't read literary biographies for

Freudian or other off-screen explanations of this or that fictional character's behaviour, loves, hatreds, late or early death. If I have strong feelings for a character in a writer's novel, I don't as a rule want to be given added information about that character by anyone other than the author (who's allowed to contribute diary-musings, if he or she likes, or proffer examples of preserved early drafts). Lengthy introductions by anyone *other* than that author I find, nowadays, a waste of time. My deep affection for Levin, in *Anna Karenina*, a man I feel sure I'd have enjoyed many an hour walking over his fields with, looking at the changing sky with, sitting on one of his long verandahs with and now and then asking him, or being asked by him, about something that is puzzling one of us, and as the evening darkened talking about this thing with, I think, plenty of pauses for reflection or for the refilling of glasses of *kvass*—anyhow, that relationship is between Levin and me, full stop. Tolstoy is, in an odd way, not far off, he may be watching us or he may have his back turned and be pondering quite other matters, but in any case nobody else is allowed near.

But that's Levin, a man who lives inside a novel, and about whom, granted that his creator has finished what he had to say about him, there is no further word that I need or want to read. Just the same words in the same order, encountered six or seven times by now, that's all I want, that's how I like it. Tolstoy himself, now, that's a different matter altogether. I've read all of his published works, and the grand ones more times than I'm sure about, and these matter more than anything else that concerns Tolstoy and me; but this doesn't mean that I'm satisfied to leave it at that. I've also read three different biographies of this world's-greatest novelist, and the reason I've done this is because my own experience in writing (pygmy-like by comparison, but you knew that already) has made it very clear to me that although my own life has provided me with many clues and direction-finders that show up in my published writings, and that although my readers can find many of those clues if they're interested enough to hunt, there remains, always and unsurprisingly, an unexplored, little-used or not used at all, but very substantial mass of images, thoughts, reflections, memories, longings, desires, acts and events and ambitions, in me, all of them in me somewhere, and the huge majority of them at rest in there, lying fallow, wordless so far, undisturbed so far, keeping perfectly still, either accidentally overlooked by me as far as using them in my published writings goes, or deliberately kept secret by me, or ignored by me…in other words, I know that there's more in me, in my history and my accessed or so-far-unaccessed mind, than any one completed piece of my work shows any sign of. There's more to come or maybe *not* to come, who knows, but it is, up until now, not visible in my work. *It's in my unknown life.*

And the only way to even begin to come closer to it would be in a biography, or, to some degree, an autobiography.

Edvard Munch dedicated his art to *"det ubevidste Sjaeleliv"*. The unknown life of the soul. I take this as a declaration of art's incompleteness (vis-à-vis the life, that is); a declaration of the fact that there are things in an artist's life which escape his or her art. Other thoughts start up from it too when I read this dedication of Munch's, but this is the first one to arrive. And I think that this, the omissions of art, the lacunae in art's gleanings from its author's life, its glints of that life but also its conscious or unconscious cloudings-over of other potential glints, is a given in the case of any artist, any artist working in any medium, any genre. A given in the case of any writer alive or dead.

I'm not forgetful of the fact that in the act of writing I often tap into images, thoughts, insights, arrangements, scenes, which are well *beyond* my normal everyday images and thoughts. Many such, and many more forays into places and events that my life has never come close to, that some might feel I haven't earned the right to speak of, where I'm riding solely on my imagination and depending on that to make up in originality and vividness for the absence of personally-observed detail. Everybody who writes even half-seriously knows that this is so. It is in fact a reason for writing, not the only reason but a big one. But it's not what I'm on at just now.

Which is, instead: literary biographies; why read them? And maybe the most telling answer to that question is the one I've touched on several paragraphs ago—that "mass" of memories and thoughts and longings that every human being has, and that writers, if they're good at their job, have probably developed, dwelt on, more than most do. Writers give us versions of this massive file on themselves, they give us edited glimpses of it, in their published works, but their lives, birth to death, if these are sensitively investigated and reported upon by others, may release further and sometimes no less moving, no less thought-worthy, lines and images and, yes, wisdom, on pages which they themselves, the novelists and poets and playwrights, either chose not to write, or didn't realize the potential beauty of if they *had* written them, or didn't find any place in their work that seemed able to house them, to give them a useable context. Or, simply, there may be things the writers forgot about until it was too late—things they didn't live long enough to use in that last book of theirs, the one they'd barely begun to glimpse the outlines of when a whole lot of things started taking those blurring and never-rescinded steps away from them.

It's why I read what I read. I'd rather read a well-managed literary biography, as long as its subject's work has mattered to me, than any Booker Prize winner's latest novel. "Well-managed" is critical here. There are superficial, fatuous, ill-written, self-promoting, paying-off-old-scores literary biographies, as there are in any category or genre of book. There are more of these than of the good ones, let alone the brilliant and moving ones. They'd be worth naming, these disgraces to the genre, in hopes of initiating a major-scale cleansing of the stables, you know the stables I mean. But not as much worth naming as what I now propose to do: which is, simply, no more dawdling, to name and talk briefly about, and as often as I can to quote from, some of the literary bios I feel most grateful to, the ones I think most about, memorize lines from most often and lend to my friends ditto, the ones I don't often re-read *in toto* but constantly re-read partially, browse in; these being books which, thanks to the biographer's invariably years'-long research, thanks also to his or her delicacy of omission and inclusion, or even, on rare occasions, thanks to a gift with language worthy of their subject, have led me up close to. And the fact is, these are lives which matter more to me than do the great majority of lives which I have shared my own allotted time in this world with.

Just one more delaying paragraph. I'm not going to list the biographies that follow in any best-first or save-best-for-last order, but I apparently do want to mention Philip Larkin again before proceeding. Larkin is the finest English-language poet of my lifetime, and since his death twenty years ago a biography has been published and I won't be mentioning it beyond what's in the next several sentences, and this absence might puzzle one or another reader, so it requires an explanation. Which is this. The biography is by the current English Poet Laureate, Andrew Motion, one of the least-gifted poets (and there've been some awfully shaky ones) ever to hold that title, and although I will agree that the author of second-or-even-eighth-rate poems *could*, yes, very conceivably write well about a great poet, I've checked this one out in a few of his ever-more-frequent appearances as critic and journalist (the laureateship obviously has done him no harm in the obtaining of these assignments) and have decided I'm not much interested in reading anything he writes; and especially do I not want to read what he has written about this poet whose work I admire so almost-unreservedly. I don't want second-or-eighth-rate sentences to clutter up my Larkin-screen. Sooner or later somebody, surely, will come along to correct this oversight, to fill in this lacuna on my literary-bio shelf; until then I'll stick with Larkin's poems and letters and the thickish file of miscellaneous stuff I have on him. In the unlikely event that this present book goes into a second edition in, say, a decade or so, and if Peter Porter or James Wood or Michael Hulse has in the meantime got it together to do the needful, then the so-far unwritten biography of Larkin which one of those men may write will lead my revised and up-dated parade.

Turns out that was only the penultimate delaying paragraph. I'll add that there are other artists/writers to whose lives the world has not yet adequately paid its debt, and among these the two I miss the most are both Scandinavians—Edvard Munch, mentioned above under 'Reviews', and Søren Kierkegaard, heretofore as wordless in this piece as one of his own several pseudonyms could have desired. Hello there, *Johannes de Silentio*. Kierkegaard I first made acquaintance with when I was living in his home town of Copenhagen, a town he rarely left and never, when he did leave, for any destination farther away than next-door Sweden or Germany (in this regard he reminds me of Larkin, who, asked if he would be interested in traveling to China or America, famously replied "Only if I could be home in time for tea."). I approached Kierkegaard via the limited Swedish I had by that time acquired (Swedish isn't interchangeable with Danish—orally the two are miles apart—but it's close enough on the page to use as a tool in moving back and forth between them), and soon arrived at a brief text called *Frygt og Boeven*. This I struggled with long enough to guess that if I were able to understand more of its sentences than I was currently managing to do, it might have seriously important things to say to me; and having, subsequently, chanced upon its author's grave (cemeteries in old towns being places I tend to spend time in) ,and having over the next several months spent a number of hours on a bench placed conveniently near that grave meditating on half-understood things, I finally and gratefully found *Frygt og Boeven's* English version, *Fear and Trembling*—which, by the way, when you look closely at 'Frygt' and remember the near fraternity of sounds among Europe's northern languages, you might wonder, as I do, why the 'Fear' of the English title is not 'Fright'. Well, onwards, but, like *Johannes de Silentio* or Philip Larkin, not far.

Kierkegaard (literally, 'Churchyard') is cryptic, is unforgivingly swift, in his writings, and let me simply say that his is a mind one should visit only at one's peril. Less tritely: you should read him only if you're prepared to have two or three of your most secure views (social, religious, political) tossed about, queried, mocked, and, very probably, by the time you're done, wrecked. But over that wreckage an unusual clarity may hover. A sharpness in the air, not like a sword but like a very keen knife, may obtrude. Kierkegaard's excursions into familiar anecdotes and belief-systems, Biblical and other, can leave these stripped and bare of their usual and accepted roles, stances, messages, and shiny with new and startlingly clear meanings. The tale of Abraham and Isaac en route to Mount Moriah becomes a koan, and the koan becomes the point of their journey. Not that Kierkegaard ever heard of a koan, he just very often thought like one.

(I don't *know* that he hadn't heard of a koan. He read more than I have done, although he had far less time in the world than I have had, so…I take it back. He may have *memorized many* koans.)

Right. Finally, now, the promised start on literary biographies, my attempt at listing and appraising for good readers books which recount the lives of writers—more *praising*, really, than *appraising*, since I believe that there are not only many such books, but many fine ones. Samuel Johnson, in the first sentence of the first of his essays published in book form as *Lives of the English Poets,* spoke of "the penury of English biography". Since Johnson was who he was, I am fairly, I am even abjectly sure that such was the case as of March 1779, when his *Lives* was first published. But it is not so now. And the proof begins with a double act, namely the same-century appearance of the two greatest dramatists of that century (the 19th primarily) and, with the single exception of Kierkegaard, the two greatest Scandanavian writers in any genre, Henrik Ibsen and August Strindberg. Michael Meyer, author of books on both these men, is one of a small number of biographers who have earned my gratitude as much as has any of their chosen subjects. This is not, of course, to say that Meyer's contribution to world-culture, to art, to me, is as great as either the Swede or the Norwegian whose names appear up there; neither of these two books of Meyer's bring the scales even remotely up to evens with *The Wild Duck* or *Miss Julie.* But this paragraph means to keep itself conscious of the "gratitude" mentioned above, and what Meyer has done is to remind me, to make vivid again in my mind, those moments in a theatre watching a play by either of these men when, thanks to them and the actors speaking their words, my mind moved in a special way, moments when my thoughts were carried close to the possibility of living, of *me* living, a profounder, truer, kinder, or braver life. Large claims, those words must seem to make, claims for feelings I seldom had during my irregular days and weeks, but could be surprised by in a theatre often enough to justify those frequent checkings of *What's On* or *Vad Händer* or whatever other form, in whatever other town or country, the rubric would take. The lines actors spoke in those moments from those stages were variously Ibsen's or Strindberg's, and I heard them and watched the lives they were representing move and come together and part and alter and return again, those changing configurations. Michael Meyer certainly watched and listened as I had, only more devotedly, more intently, and went on to spend years of his life in researching the lives of two men each of whom had, from his country on the northern fringe of a continent, written plays which changed the way theatre functioned in the western world in the late nineteenth and early twentieth centuries, and beyond that too, changed the way people thought and behaved and the way societies functioned in those years. His two biographies, written out of a sensibility I must believe both playwrights would have approved of, would perhaps, it's nice to think, have applauded from somewhere in the darkness of the dress circle, offer those lives to us with a clarity and in a detail that the plays themselves never set out to do, and, to state the obvious, do not do. They answer questions about those lives which the quality of the art that was *made* during those lives leads us to ask. The art has lifted our minds in unusual and unexpected ways and we want to know how the life and the art co-existed, how from the one the other came; we want, if we can, to understand this; perhaps, if we can understand it, it will stay with us longer. To me this wish is entirely natural and is not without a kind of dignity, there's something of a search about it, something admirable. The artist hasn't told us what we need to know in this regard, he has kept it from us, kept it away from us in the name of art, and that's all fine and good, that's as it should be, all's well with that. But it's also fine and good, and all is also 'well', with the man or woman who does this other thing. Who takes us behind the art and shows us the life.

Or so I think.

To descend now from whatever modest heights we have been on....

In my paperback copy of Michael Meyer's *Ibsen*, which I notice I bought at Heffer's in Cambridge in 1976, is this line, marked in pencil: "I have passionately longed for, yes, almost *prayed* for, a great grief which might fill my existence, give content to my life". Since I marked the line I must at that time have liked it, it must have seemed to me something like 'wisdom'. Now, though, quite a lot older, I like it less, I back off from it, shaking my head. *No, I don't want that, there are better things to pray for,* I now think, and I find myself pleased to notice that it's spoken by a *young* Ibsen, about the same age I was when I first read it and marked it as a line to come back to sometime and think further about.

It doesn't take long, though, as I read on in this biography today, before things get a whole lot better. "Is it not an indescribable joy to be able to write?" (Ibsen, in a letter to a fellow-playwright). Well, *yes.* Yes! And a few pages further on we find him, Ibsen, in Italy, he's standing in front of a Michelangelo sculpture, and the sculpture gives to him, he later writes in his journal, "a new standard to aim at". Which makes me want to say again (would shouting be too much? too…theatrical?) *Yes, Yes*, and I want to add a line or two now, I want to say something which however obvious can hardly be said or acted upon too often: namely, that great art, great music or a great painting or a great novel or poem or play, offers *standards* which, if that art is accessible, if we live (yes, I mean *literally—metaphorically* isn't bad but is second-best here) near it, near enough to that gallery or that concert-house that we can get to it fairly often, if we see that marvelous building even half-awarely on our customary daily peregrinations, or listen to that piece of music often, *often*, probably without acknowledging how much a part of our daily life it has become—*or if we read about the people who built or painted or wrote them*—this can matter. Yes. "And *how*", as I was wont to say a lot of years ago. And *how* it can matter.

More than merely 'matter', really, but I'll stand back a bit and trust that that will show itself in what follows.

Which reminds me of Gertrude Stein saying, a long while ago, from her home in Paris, "America will be a good place for writers someday, but not yet". A saying which a surprising—well, not so surprising—number of today's North American writers seem either to know or to have thought about and then acted on all on their own, whether they admit that this is what they're doing or not. They tend not to admit it but they tend to do it. And no, I'm not talking about Hemingway and Fitzgerald and the celebrated 1920s, all that. I'm talking about today, right now, I'm referring to the fact that a great many writers from this country or the one to the south of us, spend half of every year in Europe, so that they can stand, metaphorically speaking now, in front of a Michelangelo.

Not really a digression, that. It's the same instinct at work as the one which leads some of them, these writers and artists, not to far-off places, but to literary biographies. To read about other lives, other times, other cultures.

Back to *Ibsen*, and another of the worth-remembering paragraphs with which Meyer's book is richly provided. "There is a fact, and for me a strange fact, about the really great artists of the past. In some way their late works become simplified and fragmentary, become imperfect and unfinished. The artists stop caring about beauty and such things, and yet their works get better."

My point in quoting that is that it's *not* Ibsen speaking here, it's the sculptor Henry Moore. And it is Michael Meyer whose far-ranging mind brings these lines to us, lines which, having never before shared a page with anything Ibsenish, can bring us to an unexpected halt and thoughtfulness in a section where Meyer is dealing with the play *When We Dead Awaken*, a late and, yes, flawed Ibsen work. It's the kind of *trouvaille* that will distinguish the truly gifted biographer from the slogger, from the writer who churns books of this genre out on a near-annual basis, the Henri Troyats and Jeffrey Meyerses and others one could name. It's an example of the level Meyer at his best can reach, and it is, perhaps, a sufficient reason for starting this essay off with him.

The difference between *Ibsen* and *Strindberg* (the books, not the men), surprises me on this rereading. The terrain, if I may put it so, of the two lives, both lives lived for the most part in Scandinavia, is so different! Ibsen's life is touching, familiar, recognizable, and full of poetry, as are his plays; Strindberg's is dramatic, all *Sturm und Drang*, although also, as it goes on, not less moving, and not less a generous stimulus and idea-sparkle for the receptive mind. Look at Strindberg's paintings, which I saw exhibitions of in both Sweden and Denmark and which I think to be as powerful as those of any other northern painter*, whether Scandinavian or Canadian; they are clearly by the same 'tortured', pardon the cliché, artist as the author of *Miss Julie* and *The Father* and *The Ghost Sonata*.

Here are some lines that stay with me from this second of Meyer's Scandinavian biographies. From a Paris review of *Miss Julie* : "Ibsen's work is shot through with poetry. M.Strindberg by contrast seems to wish to ban poetry from his theatre, eject it as something dangerously seductive and unworthy of one whose mind is full of bitter truths."

Here's Strindberg writing a letter during a sojourn in Austria: "This is happiness…sitting in a hut on the Danube among six women who regard me as a semi-idiot, and knowing that in Paris, the intellectual center of the world, 500 people are sitting in an auditorium

---

*barring, need it be said, Edvard Munch

silent as mice, stupid enough to expose their brains to my power of suggestion."

Again, "Bachelor life strikes me as dirty. Family life is the most beautiful—but! but! even dirtier when one stirs it."

Also, "One's longing for purity and beauty manifests itself most strongly after sinning. It is strange. Is this the purpose of sin?"

And finally, "As soon as I have pen and paper ready, it starts to flow. The words pour forth and my pen has to work at full pressure to get it all down…I have the sensation that I am hovering freely in space. It is as though a higher will than mine causes the pen to glide across the paper and write words that come to me from without…"

Quick switch now to one of the many, many fine women literary-biographers: they include Hermione Lee for her marvellous *Virgina Woolf*, Fiona MacCarthy for her superlative 800-page *William Morris*, Victoria Glendinning's carefully researched *Trollope,* and Claire Tomalin's *Pepys* (one brief paragraph from this last, much the freshest news of Pepys that we've had since his Diaries first appeared: here Tomalin has been telling us of "Betty Michell" daughter of a London shopkeeper and one whom Pepys first saw as a little girl and watched as she grew into adolescence and determined to have, and did have; and then ceased to desire and the connection dwindled and ended. After she leaves the Diary's pages we know, of course, nothing more of her. Tomalin writes, "But Betty Michell…disappears into the darkness of unrecorded history, with her fading childish beauty, her dressing box, her sullen husband in his spirit shop beside the Thames and her second baby girl, whose fate we shall never know; having freed herself of uncle Pepys and sublimely unaware of the literary honour bestowed on her by him.").

Tomalin has also done Shelley, Mansfield, and Wollstonecraft, all three accounts clear as spring-water. And Thomas Hardy, published just months ago.

But the one I'm switching to now is Brenda Maddox, whose *Nora,* Joyce's Nora of course, is a better-managed biography, if you ask me, than the celebrated Richard Ellmann's life of Nora's husband. (Richard Ellman, whether writing of Joyce or of Wilde, seems to me painstaking and decades-taking, and densely accurate without much air or light. I think most people would disagree with this.)

Brenda Maddox brings both Nora and James to generous life, and patronizes neither of them. Yes, Nora's letters are not rich in classical allusions or even in grammar, but the passion, the anger, the commonsense—! It's entirely clear, now, having read this book, as it was never clear in Ellman, what the two of them, James and Nora, had going for them: it wasn't all praiseworthy (prominent in it was possessiveness, ill temper, flying crockery) but it gives off the energy that I remember (a frivolous analogy, this, but it occurred to me so I'm going with it) from the Woodstock (Ont.) CNR station of my childhood when, as often happened, by some scheduling mess-up there were engines standing on both the coming and the going sides, and the two engines were panting steam out over the entire little town. "I feel much better since last night", Nora worries in a letter when she's in Ireland and James is home in their flat in Trieste, "but feels (sic) a bit lonely tonight as it is so wet I was reading your letters all day as I had nothing else to do…"; and then, at the end of that letter (more movingly revealing than anything to be found in that door-stopper of Ellman's), "I suppose you will be lighting the fire when you get this".

Nora worried about prostitutes when James was anywhere on his own and he wrote back to assure her she could supply "all and more" that/than those women could. Her letters were seldom saved but James quoted so slavishly from them that one can, as Maddox says, easily reconstruct them. To say that their correspondence is naked is all too easy, it's a temptation I ought to have resisted. Maddox writes: "She was so short of money, she said, that she was going around without underclothes."

There is a lot of that in *Nora*, nothing was left unmentioned except the proprieties, but there is also much sadness. Aside from the damage they both incurred in their needy and isolated togetherness, their daughter's unhappy life and death and their son's inglorious career are also now in the public domain. Along that line there is much that can interest and undoubtedly has interested Joycean scholars, although nothing remotely at the sometimes-enlightening, some-times-murky depth of Ellman's work. Nora never read *Ulysses*: this is, writes Maddox, "her best-known fault", but, Maddox adds, "she shares it with most of the human race".

You may know of Brenda Maddox from her more-recent book on the woman who ought to have had a share in a Nobel Prize and was cheated out of it by those who did get that prize: Rosalind Franklin, *The Dark Lady of DNA*. Not a literary biography, that one, but it's on my shelves anyway. A darker and more soberly managed book it is, and Rosalind a greatly different central figure of that story than Nora of hers.

What's next? From the pile of books on the floor by my desk, I pick *Diderot*, by P.N. Furbank, the latter better known through his first and best-loved biographee, E..M. Forster.What did I know of Diderot until I read this Life? Something about the Encyclopedists and the *Éclaircissment*, is all. No, one thing more, I had read *Le Neveu de Rameau*, because somewhere I had heard that this was one of France's finest short books, and since another short French book, *Adolphe*, was then and has ever afterwards remained close to my heart, I had checked it out.

Not really close to the pared-down, incised quality of *Adolphe*, I had decided, but OK. Furbank, though, brought me more interesting sounds from Diderot than *Le Neveu de Rameau* had provided. Of a lover who failed him in some unspecified regard: "Madame, take care; you are disfiguring yourself in my heart". Of Diderot's reputation as a star at the Encyclopedists' gatherings, Furbank writes: "There are many descriptions, more than one by himself, of his dazzling improvisations and ardent tirades at d'Holbach's table." And again, "He was careless of his own intellectual property and equally careless of others', a trait which sometimes got him into serious trouble. (It went with that habit of his, when carried away in talk, of gripping his interlocutor's body as if it belonged to him.)"

And here is a kind of wisdom-sentence, or so I think it to be; that there are many such in this book is why I am as fond of both Furbank and his subject as I am. "Friendship, for him, was of supreme importance and an imperative duty for mankind; and in his *Letter on the Deaf and Dumb* he praises the law of the ancient Scythians which required all citizens to have at least one friend, allowed them to have two, and forbade them three."

On the basis of everything else I learn from this book of Diderot and his "dazzling improvisations", I'm not at all sure that the ancient

Scythians ever thought of such a requirement. But if they didn't it is a very great fault in them, and I am glad to have this fault brought, late as it may be, into the open.

Of a certain Marquis, whose wit, Diderot thought, was the most delicate and unmalicious he had ever known—"It was like brandy-flames…running all over my head without burning a hair".

His friends said of him that he "could see a hundred brilliant things in a work but not the ones that actually happened to be there". Which reminds me of Kenneth Tynan's theatre reviews in *The Observer* in the late 1950s. His enemies, who were legion, would hint he hadn't seen the play he was reviewing at all. Who cared?—his columns were brilliant, firing off similes like meteor-showers. I'd settle for Diderot/ Tynan's sort of 'seeing' anytime.

Of the painter Boucher, Diderot wrote, "That man only takes up his brush to show me tits and buttocks. Now, I am more than happy to see such things, but I cannot bear to have somebody pointing them out to me."

And now and then, in this biography, it occurs to me that what I am responding to in such an all-at-once way is that I am quite often being reminded of myself. Aside from the matter of genius, I damn-well better add. For instance there is someone with whom Diderot is in heated correspondence and to whom Diderot has sent a letter written during the whole of a day and a night, and who writes back at once and at equal length; Diderot then writes begging him to slow down, the pace of the correspondence, he says, is killing him. Which reminds me of receiving, some dozen years ago, an e-mail from a friend imploring me to answer *her* emails less rapidly, she's made to feel guilty if she doesn't answer mine just as fast. Neither of us has written since.

Well, some sort of similarity seemed to be there.

Furbank draws towards a close with this. Diderot, he writes, "was one of those mortals who are endowed by nature or destiny with a whole array of virtues and talents. His addiction to self-praise finds its justification here, it being a continual and beautiful surprise to him what precious qualities, what capacities for ardent feeling or original thought, he has discovered in himself. This was no occasion for vanity, for he might just as easily have had the misfortune to have been born an imbecile."

I'm interpolating a line here which has very little to do with Diderot other than that it was spoken of a contemporary of his, Jean-Jacques Rousseau, by yet another Frenchman to whom I owe plenty: Stendhal. The latter wrote, of Rousseau, that he "was unhappy all his life because he sought the kind of friend of which ten or so, perhaps, have existed from Homer's time until ours".

"*Ça donne à penser*", as French-speaking persons have been known to murmur to themselves from time to time

Back to Furbank. He has written, also, the biography of one of my own almost-privately-owned, as I like to think, writers. This is Italo Svevo, Joyce's friend during his Trieste years. Svevo wrote all his life but publication was always long-delayed and recognition arrived inadequately even at the end. His Zeno is close to Gogol's Oblomov, another personal (although less private) favourite, a character almost as dilatory as Zeno, almost as willing to remain forever outside the spotlight's circle. Here's Svevo: "When you are old you have to stay in the shade, however witty you are". Do I know anyone who has composed a sentence that is at once more truthful and half as wry as that? I do not.

Furbank's breakthrough book is probably *E.M.Forster: A Life*, a book bursting, quietly, with roadsigns intended to direct the reader towards his or her own shimmering-in-the-distance life. "He always believed himself incapable of abstract thought", Furbank writes of Forster (this is, I think, a not-uncommon circumstance among writers although one that is not always acknowledged). Other characteristics compensated. An aunt said of him at five "any pleasure for him is I am sure double what it is to other people."

Here is an excerpt from pages written on his return from his first time in Italy, pages entitled '*an evening walk in the Campagna*'. "They were walking together in the blue dusk, and all I saw is that their age was about twenty and their shirts not the same colour. They had their arms around each other's necks, as English youths have….They turned behind the embankment and I have not seen them again, nor shall I know them if I do. Perhaps they parted in bitterness round the corner over a half lira loan, but to me they are Orestes and Pylades, always young, always beautiful, always giving the truest blessing—the blessing of those who know not that they give."

And here, à *propos* Forster in his twenties. "Something had shifted in his soul, and energies he had only half-glimpsed in himself were now in his possession. For all the tameness of his outward existence, he was able, imaginatively, to respond to the 'greatness' of life. When his friends read his first books, what surprised them was their vigour and largeness. They had expected a book by him to be charming …ineffectual…So far he had not felt 'important'. Now he did so, having trusted the imagination."

Back in England after another Italian sojourn, "not for the first time, he felt its genteel comedies and atrocities." And, " It was 'monstrous' to like such people" Forster wrote, "Sympathy too has its dangers. Follow either passionate love or truth—the latter purifies invisibly."

Lastly, from his *Commonplace Book*, 1943, "Wisdom, when acquired, proves incommunicable and goes with our learning into the grave. The edges of it occasionally impinge on people, though, and strike a little awe into them."

So much that has gone into the grave!—so much, also, that can impinge, that can even "strike a little awe". Here, from Fiona MacCarthy's 780-page biography of William Morris, the 'pre-Raphaelite' painter, poet, novelist, fabric-and-tapestry designer, architect, builder, social reformer, traveller, explorer, are a few lines that alone make this glitteringly intelligent book worth its impressive weight. "He had his own link with the prehistoric landscape. The giant horse cut out of chalk in the Berkshire Downs aroused strong emotions in him. He [made annual pilgrimages to it, and] even went to see it, by then in flagging health, in the year before his death. He could summon up past scenes, re-people empty landscapes, with an almost lunatic exactness: *Not seldom I please myself,* he wrote, *with trying to realize the face of mediaeval England; the many chases and great woods, the stretches of common tillage and common pasture quite unenclosed…*"

"It is essentially a cinematic vision", MacCarthy writes, and "Had he lived a little later, he might have been an Eisenstein."

Morris once asked himself the rhetorical question ("the question from a fairytale", says MacCarthy, with those five words showing her credentials for inclusion in anybody's library) 'what did he consider the thing most to be longed for'. His immediate reply was "a beautiful House", and he continued, "and if I were further asked to name the thing next to be longed for, I should answer, A beautiful Book".

Near his home at Kelmscott were, he wrote, "some half-dozen tiny village churches, every one of which is a beautiful work of art." What he found most moving about these churches, MacCarthy writes, "was their apparent spontaneity, *arrived at because of their directness of intention*." My italics there—my bit of learning from that day's reading in this biography. What to do with that italicized phrase, beyond simply admiring and quoting it? Well, for starters it re-fortifies my mind with thoughts of Thomas Hardy, of Edward Thomas, of the 'peasant-poet' John Clare, of D.H.Lawrence—all of them writers whose persuasive powers derive, I think, from a 'directness of inten-tion' which, having picked up the phrase from this Life, having deliberated upon it and found that it 'worked', it was honest and valuable, I have more than a few times benefited from while trying to add strength or clarity to this or that poem or page.

Morris's daughter Jenny lived until 1935, unhappy and confused for many of her last years. Near the end of her long life she would sometimes be found wandering in the garden (at Kelmscott): "I often walk here in the evening hoping to meet my dear father, he was such a sweet companion".

And that garden-image I include here for no reason other than the great pleasure and the even greater sadness of finding it.

MacCarthy has also a fine *Byron, Life and Legend*, a book from which her subject emerges with unexpected (by me) credit: not just the panache and swagger we all know about, but, in addition to that, an intelligence easily superior to the gaggle of poets and hangers-on with whom he's usually associated. His mind seems to have moved impatiently and easily from, let's say, debauchery, to a flight among images the rest of them would have sold their estates or their often-paltry MSS for. Venice, before he'd ever seen it, was "the greenest island of my imagination"; and later, describing English tourists in that town when he was making his home there, he wrote of "that parcel of staring boobies, who go about gaping and wishing to be at once cheap and magnificent."

His journals and letters vibrate with energy, he impressed some of the greatest and, I'd have thought, hardest-to-impress minds of his century (Flaubert, that world-mocker, writes of him like a dazzled schoolboy, telling us that when he visited Chillon he looked for and found Byron's name written on a stone there, and "…the stone is slightly eaten away, as if the mighty hand that leant there had worn it away with its weight.")

He was "dangerous to look at", Lady Liddell told her daughter, advising her to keep her eyes elsewhere if he were in the room.

Here's a nickel's-worth of advice for anyone who reads this essay and considers using it as a source, a tip-sheet, of names and titles of literary biographies. I hope you'll find many to your taste, and it occurs to me that, amidst the praisings of which there are many here, it's appropriate to include the occasional warning, the occasional heads-up and hands-off. The heads-up/hands-off here is simply this, that in my experience double-barrelled Lives—a second volume which usually follows some years after the first—is often a barrel too many. This may simply be because the middle and later years of the biographee lack the energy that he or she had when young; it may be because the doubts and false starts and, yes, the youthful loves and losses, have been replaced by a tedious listing of honours and achievements; it may also be that the biographer's interest in his subject flags. For whatever reason, the falling-off is plain in the case of Nicholas Boyle's Goethe double-header, the first of which kept me on the look-out for the second for five years, it was so fine, so life-expansive, so revelatory of the culture of that entire language-area of central Europe. Vol.II was therefore bought the first day it was in the shops, hard-cover price and all. A bad idea: the mature Goethe, Privy Councillor to that small dukedom in provincial Germany, dutiful husband to a boring wife and re-visitor at the fading sites of his youthful triumphs, is no fun to be with, has no new tales to tell, and Boyle spends far too many pages on him without appearing to notice this. Five-cent advice: buy and read the first, borrow and browse the second.

Same thing, although less obviously, with Richard Holmes's Coleridge two-parter. The first, *Coleridge: Early Visions*, is as fine as biography gets: James Wood (in, where else, *The Guardian*—Wood gets all the plum reviewing-assignments there) says of it that it has "the aura of fiction, the shimmer of an authentic portrait", and I can't improve on or quarrel with that.

A few examples of the aura and the shimmer. A schoolteacher of the young Coleridge "showed no mercy to phrase, metaphor, or image, unless supported by sound sense", the teen-ager wrote of him. Good on you, teacher. Again, writing from Cambridge, Coleridge describes hauling a drunken fellow-undergraduate out of the shallow gutter in King's Parade, the while the drunk insisted that he save his friend instead, crying "Never mind me—I can swim."

Of his friendship with Charles Lamb: "Long alcoholic evenings passed effortlessly away in the tavern snug, fuelled by egg-flip and clouds of tobacco, while they exchanged new sonnets and emotional intimacies of their tortured love-lives."

And here's a quotation I hadn't seen before: "The poet is a metaphysician who actively engages with nature, who goes out of himself, who *hunts down* the otherness of being…"

He had a close friend and sometime-patron at Stowey in Somerset named Tom Poole. This startling news reaches you because I had a great-grandfather named Clement Poole Coles, whose mother had been a Poole who also lived in Stowey. Tom and Sam may have together taken "a night expedition to listen to the nightingales in a grove of trees just north of Holford-Stower coaching road". Drunk beyond caution by thoughts of that probable-relative and that expedition and those nightingales, I will now go on to tell you that while on sabbatical and renting a largeish house in Cambridge in 1979, our next-door neighbour's maiden name was Sara Coleridge, and on the walls of her livingroom were paintings of two of her ancestors, one of these S.T. Coleridge and the other Sir Philip Sidney. Sara was a beautiful woman who rode, probably spectacularly, to hounds, and cared little for poetry. Is this news worth inclusion here?

I think so, or I wouldn't've.

Vol.II, *Darker Reflections,* is not as markedly inferior to its predecessor as was the case with Boyle's *Goethe* Mark Two, but Coleridge's well-known depressions and dejections do, as its title warns us, darken its pages. Just one borrowing from it: Coleridge was announced to be giving a series of lectures at the Royal Institution, and did give the first several of these, to considerable acclaim, but either broke down or, if his own account was true, had his lecture-notes stolen en route to the Institution and could for this reason not perform; in any case, the Institution did not permit him to give any further lectures. These remaining lectures, Richard Holmes cheerfully writes, were delivered by "the Reverend Mr.Dibdin, otherwise unknown to fame".

Before leaving Richard Holmes: his *Shelley, The Pursuit*, is right up there with *Early Visions*. Here he is (Shelley, not Holmes) on the moral function of poetry: "The great secret of morals is love, or a going out of our own nature and an identification with the beautiful....A man, to be greatly good, must imagine intensely and comprehensively; he must put himself in the place of another and of many others..." The last thirteen words there may be found just about verbatim in Rilke's *Letters to a Young Poet*.

Back to the perils of the two-parter. These would have to include Robert Gittings's two books on Thomas Hardy; and, an exception to this after-all-rather-pliant Law, Brian Boyd's 600-and-800-pagers on Nabokov. The last-named is stupendous in its scope and detail; written well, I think, though not with quite the genial Holmesian touch. It's true that if Nabokov is your subject, you needn't be witty yourself, the wit will flow endlessly and effortlessly from your main man. Main *person*, of course, yes, yes.

Just a few examples:

Of those who wear or own jewellery, Nabokov pretends to admire their "hilarious atavistic regard for precious minerals".

In another mode, and oddly close to Wilfred Owens's 1918 often-quoted "the beauty is in the pity", there's Nabokov 's "Beauty plus pity is the closest we can get to a definition of art."

He loved his father, who died throwing himself between an assassin's bullet and its intended target at a political meeting in Berlin; loved his mother too, and wrote, this brilliant satirist and ironist, the following note to her on the third anniversary of the death of that husband/father. "Three years have gone—and every trifle relating to father is still as alive as ever inside me. I am so certain, my love, that we will see him again, in an unexpected but completely natural heaven, in a realm where all is radiance and delight. He will come towards us in our common bright eternity, slightly raising his shoulders as he used to do, and we will kiss the birthmark on his hand without surprise. You must live in expectation of that tender hour, my love, and never give in to the temptation of despair. Everything will return…"

Nabokov is a magician, and language is his wand. Leaving Boyd to one side for a moment: *Pale Fire*, a short novel with an ageing poet as a central figure, contains one of that poet's poems (it is, of course, a Nabokov poem): the poem, long and precisely rhyming and embedded in a novel as unsentimental and mocking as any novel can be, is as moving as anything in poetry. Read it and fail to weep, if you can.

(Nabokov greatly admired A.E. Housman, another whose poetry once moved many and now, apparently, moves only a few. Moves me, though, which counts a lot inside this essay. Interesting to wonder how Housman would feel about Nabokov. He'd admire *Pale Fire*, the poem-inside-the-novel, although he'd probably dislike everything else about the novel. As for *Lolita*…I don't think so.)

Boyd does well with his colossal assignment. After a last Nabokovian interjection, I'll leave them both. "There are three points of view from which a writer can be considered; he may be considered as a storyteller, as a teacher, as an enchanter. A major writer combines these three—storyteller, teacher, enchanter—but it is the enchanter in him that predominates and makes him a major writer." In his teaching at Wellesley, the women's college in New England where this Russian who made himself a writer in his birth-country's language, then a writer in German, and finally, of course, a writer in English, spent a good many of his middle years, Nakokov invariably explained, in the first lecture of the course he taught, that 'enchantment' always came from detail. His example would be a "quite incidental" messenger in a Dickens story who when paid for his errand "receives his twopence with anything but transport, tosses the money into the air, catches it over-handed, and retires." This one gesture, with its epithet "over-handed", Nabokov would explain to his class, is "a trifle…but because of this trifle the man is alive forever in a good reader's mind".

Which reminds one of Chekhov and his advice not to describe the river in its broad night-time flow, but to mention, instead, the scrap of moonlight reflecting on the neck of an empty bottle floating out there….

And here comes another Russian and one who is, in the context of this article, an oddity: oddity because I have never read any of his poetry that has mattered a jot, whatever a jot is, to me. Of course I've 'read him' (I'm speaking of, it might be a good idea to mention this, Alexander Pushkin) in translation, but always come up short in terms of admiration, of emotion, in any terms at all except the self-congratulation that I've once again made my laborious way through whatever the poem is—*Eugene Onegin*, usually. So why is Pushkin here? Two reasons: first, because I've read two biographies of this phenomenon, this descendant of an African slave of the Russian Tsar, and I find his life both moving and, Nabokovian term, enchanting. Secondly, and probably more persuasively, he's here because he is acknowledged by every Russian from Chekhov to Nabokov to, so far as I know, the humblest Russian reader, as the greatest poet in the history of the language, and I have no problem in taking that universal acknowledgement, that verdict of the writers and readers of All the Russias, seriously. He *must* be, it's as simple as that, a great poet. He must also be, lamentably, an untranslatable poet. Many translations of poetry, if you can read even imperfectly the language in which the poet wrote it as well as the now-Englished version—whether it be Rilke or Cavafy or Baudelaire or Tranströmer—at least give you a clear signal that here is something fine, here are lines that can, even through the mangled rhythms and lost rhymes of the hobbling original (because nothing is ever *equal* in this game), speak to you, show you a scene or a sound that is almost important, hint at what they really are behind the mask. Not so with Pushkin. So we're left with the life, and all I will do here is offer a few glimpses of that life.

Pushkin loved poetry and women. He was, my two biographers (they are Elaine Feinstein and T.J. Binyon, and each has done a good job with her or his man) agree, not handsome; Binyon says he was downright ugly. He was 5'6" tall, black curly hair, broad nose, blue eyes, 'offensive' to some women in "the blatancy of his sexual need"; and he had many lovers, all of them female; and his wife was a famous beauty. Does any of that add up? Well, yes. He was neither wealthy nor given to aesthetic posturings: when he was halfway through writing *Onegin* he wrote to a friend "Fuck fame, it's money I need". But when he was living in Odessa an older man, a former Vice-

Governor of the province, became his friend and wrote of him that "his conversation was like electricity making contact with the black preoccupations inside me", and again, "Often, in the midst of some idle, amusing talk, a bright new idea flew from his soul which astonished me with the wide range of his intelligence", and, last words from this ex-Vice-Governor, "Little by little I discovered a whole buried treasure of sound reasoning and noble ideas, which he concealed under a soiled cloak of cynicism."

It's what you keep on finding people saying about Alexander Pushkin. He was, I'm persuaded, and never mind if I can't value his poetry as I ought, obviously an ever-burning fire of talent, of energy, of wit, of words that pretty well anyone who came close to him couldn't resist and didn't forget. That's not quite true. Pushkin craved company and laughter and talk and drink and…well, probably he was always looking about to find and connect with as much in the way of fellow-genius as his vast homeland could offer. Whereas his wife, the beauteous and sexy Natalya, had other interests. Pushkin was, up to a point, prepared for those interests, he often wrote to friends that he didn't expect happiness, that 'domestic sorrow' was something he had 'made allowance for' when he married; but he was no complaisant husband, and when he thought a fellow-officer was becoming a nuisance in this regard, he challenged him to a duel and was shot. Lying in his library where he'd been carried by his second and his doctor, he said "Something is weighing me down", and died. He was 37 years old.

There's not another writer I know anything of, certainly none of the many others named in this book, who seems to me to have had more of the much-mentioned 'sacred fire' glowing in him or her than the walking and talking conflagration that this 'ugly' man obviously, *obviously*, was. Who wouldn't want to have known him? Reading either Binyon or Feinstein is the closest you can get to that fire now.

Unless, of course, you can read Russian.

Who's next? There are a number of people, and among them are most of my all-time favourite writers, who still await their true, their comprehensive, their necessary biographer. This is a baffling lack, but it's so. These writers are: Albert Camus, Robert Musil, George Eliot, and Leo Tolstoy. And Thomas Mann. And Edvard Munch, although, as you will be thinking, he's no writer at all.

Camus was #1 in the world for me through the later half of my college years, I knew *L'Étranger*'s first several pages by heart *in French*, my copy was as well-thumbed and dog-eared as any book I've ever owned, and when a Frenchwoman called Annette to whom I loaned it at a party in London one night in 1955 never returned my calls or my Camus, it was the missing book I grieved hardest over. I've never lost my strong sense of closeness with its author, although as far as *L'Étranger* is concerned, I've known for a long while that I like a later novel of his, *La Chute,* more.

A biography of Camus is briefly discussed elsewhere in this book. It would be nice if a well-written one would appear within my lifetime. Fairly soon would be best.

Musil, author of *The Man Without Qualities,* a multi-volume unfinished novel which is what Marcel Proust might have written if he had been heterosexual, as Musil beyond all reasonable doubt was, can also be said to be the author of one of the very rare, maybe the *only* book that I sometimes imagine I might (had I been born into a well-off Austrian family about the turn of the last century, and had I had the stamina of this hard-exercising, super-fit man, and had I had, possibly, one or two other features/gifts that were his and may not be mine) have written. I don't know if that sentence got finished in time for you—what it says is that there's hardly a line in this immensely long novel that I feel is alien to me, that I don't respond to pretty intimately. That's unusual. I typically read it in English although I possess the original text, *Der Mann Ohne Eigenschaften,* and can say that, testing the quality of the translation here and there, I have found it generally OK.

Except for the title. '*Eigenschaften*' doesn't really do well as 'qualities': the word itself is more nearly translated as 'attributes', although 'eigen' means 'own' in the sense of 'one's own', something unique to oneself. Either 'qualities ' or 'attributes' would just scrape by in the title if the whole of it is understood ironically, but that, to one who hasn't read the book, cannot be counted on. As things stand, a 'man without qualities' might, to an Anglophone reader, be a man without much value or worth, but what Musil is presenting us with in this unfinished novel is a protagonist (Ulrich) who is highly intelligent, does well at everything (and with every individual, man or woman) he touches, is obviously attractive to men as friend or counsellor and to women as either of those things and/or lover, and whose career-choices have varied interestingly from adolescence on, with evident gifts for, and, on his part, dissatisfactions with, every one of those choices. What Ulrich is 'without', or lacks, is a willingness to commit or limit himself to any one profession or life-path—no sooner does he begin to test one of these out than its absurdities overwhelm him. As a result, the congeries of noblemen, cabinet members, generals and business tycoons who are his acquaintances and all of whom, with scarcely a single exception, Musil and Ulrich both mock, find Ulrich baffling, are insecure in his company, privately acknowledge him to be their intellectual superior (and probably, they suspect, better in bed), and to protect themselves tend to keep their distance.

So this is *not* a man without 'qualities'. It's not, either, a man without 'attributes'. Just possibly the word that is his *own* (i.e., *eigen*) here—that which he is 'without'—is 'certainties', or possibly 'commitments' or possibly, an extreme solution with its own new set of difficulties, 'faiths'.

The longer I go on with this the more I understand the translators' probable despair. Sufficient perhaps to say that Musil awaits his title just as he awaits his biographer. In the latter regard a door-stopper of a book does exist, in German, and I own it, but the 50-odd pages of this that I've read really, really lowered my spirits. Naming it here would do none of us good.

Enough of Robert Musil. He should be read as much as Proust is read, although possibly by a different readership. He's sly, is deeply versed in *entre-deux-guerres* central European history, is funny, and has some of the subtlest sexual byplay in his great (and unfinished— he died, this confident fitness-fanatic, well ahead of his self-predicted death-date, leaving 1370 small-print pages of his novel and over a thousand additional even-smaller-print pages entitled 'afterthoughts' and 'further afterthoughts' and 'new afterthoughts') story that I know of anywhere. I mean that it's subtle and funny once you catch onto it, I don't mean that it's either of those things in the way that some people think Philip Roth is subtle or funny. Musil's never repetitive or one-track and he's hardly at all predictable.

Tolstoy I should probably just leave alone. He's as great as Shakespeare, nothing original in saying so, and no other writer is close to either of them, and although there's some excuse for the lack of a great biography of Shakespeare*, there's none in the case of Tolstoy**. Troyat tried, A.N.Wilson tried, there must be others and I may have read them, but nothing's been good enough to put this anomaly to rest.

George Eliot is a similar case, i.e. there's nothing worthy of getting this article's *imprimatur* in her case either. There exists a quite recent and energetic attempt entitled *George Eliot, The Last Victorian* by Kathryn Hughes, which is likeable but neither detailed nor learned enough; and there's a plodding one by a Yale professor named Gordon S. Haight. So the finest of all English-language novelists—'finest' not just because of *Middlemarch* but also thanks to Part One of *Daniel Deronda* (the Cambridge don F.R. Leavis, whose lectures I used long ago to show up at the Mill Street lecture-rooms to listen to much more regularly than I listened to my own tutor's vapourings, insisted in one of those strident but mind-reformatting hours that the brilliant Part One of this novel should be entitled *Gwendolen Harleth* and published and admired separately, with Part II, *Daniel Deronda,* left to sermonize and flounder on its own. The special appeal of this new arangement would then be that its author's insights, the unique solemnity of her judgements, could reach her readers unmarred by her didactic obsession, at that time, with Judaism. It would then be as if, chortled Leavis from his podium, the egregious Rev. Casaubon could be excised from *Middlemarch* and we could head straight on towards Dorothea's hungered-after trysting with Will Ladislaw, also towards Lydgate's gradual subsidence towards "the succubus Rosamond", towards Fred Vincy and Mary Garth and Bulstrode and the whole entirely adequate rest of that marvelous novel's cast)—is still left waiting for her *Life*. And so are we all.***

---

*Although Stephen Greenblatt's *Will in the World* will do nicely until one comes along.

**There's a skillfully colloquial new translation of *War and Peace* by Anthony Briggs, just out last year.

***I've been waiting for the right place to insert a—not a *caveat*, really, but a

Among George Eliot's contemporaries were Thomas and Jane Carlyle, and there's a recent and highly readable account of that bittersweet, more bitter than sweet, marriage in a book entitled *Thomas and Jane Carlyle, Portrait of a Marriage*, by Rosemary Ashton. Here's a brief snapshot from that *Portrait*. Ashton tells us that in writing a brief *Life* of his "gifted but unfulfilled" friend John Sterling, Carlyle described "without pomp" his own role in that life and added without comment Sterling's dying letter to him, but withheld the stanzas addressed personally to him, because, he said, "these were 'written as if in star-fire and immortal tears; which are among my sacred possessions, to be kept for myself alone."

To be kept for *what*? For himself alone? *Not* sold to the tabloids for a half-million quid, or mailed off to the *TLS* or the *LRB* for a fortnight of personal puffery? Once in a while one or another Victorian can still lift us into a moment bearing a trace of unmockable class with it....

Two quite different biographies of Samuel Beckett appeared almost simultaneously a few years ago, the scholarly 1996 *Damned to Fame* by James Knowlson and the stylish 1997 *Samuel Beckett, The Last Modernist*, by Anthony Cronin. I read both and finally couldn't decide (since both are richly informative and both by writers who love the man they write of) which was the one to make my honour-roll here. You now know how this dilemma was resolved. Just one comment on an oddity to be found on page 148 of Cronin's book. Speaking of a play Beckett assisted in producing in Paris, a play called *La Souriante Madame Beudet*, Cronin bafflingly writes, "Like Madame Bovary, Madame Beudet murders her husband..." Well, his editors ought to be running for cover right alongside him.)

We're drawing to a close now, and I'll hurry things along by simply listing the dozen or so absolutely must-read books still unmentioned.

[cont'd...] kind of shotgun-rider that I think should accompany this essay, should be somewhere visible as the essay heads out towards whereever it's going. It's a quotation from the fine biographer Victoria Glendinning, who writes this in her book on Jonathan Swift: "'I'm inclined to think', Joe Orton wrote in his diary, 'that the main fascination of Swift (as with Dylan Thomas, Brendan Behan and many other writers and artists) is with his life.' Maybe.", adds Glendinning, "But if were not for the work, none of these would have had the lives that they did."

Here's one, a biography of another of my younger self's heroes, *Cyril Connolly, A Life*, by Jeremy Lewis. Connolly's elegiac collection, *The Unquiet Grave*, published under the pseudonym 'Palinurus' in his own magazine *Horizon* in 1944, was a kind of Bible for me for, maybe, too many years; 'too many' because it isn't and never was, I daresay, the most grownup, true-wisdom sort of handbook that I took it for. Palinurus is the name of Aeneas's steersman on the last lap of their long voyage, the lap from Carthage to Rome, and near the end of that journey he drowsed at the wheel and fell into the sea and was drowned. Connolly adopted his name as a symbolic admission of his own life's inertia and loss of direction. That's a sense of self that I didn't exactly have or deserve but liked the idea that one day I might have it. Anyhow I loved the little book and still see it on its shelf with special feelings.

Connolly's mentioned at more length in the memoir to be found further in, deeper down.

OK, then there's Tim Hilton's two-parter on John Ruskin, quite wonderful; another is or are Ray Monk's two books, *Ludwig Wittgenstein* and *Bertrand Russell* (not really writers *pur laine,* I know; still, they wrote a bit, and Monk does well with them); Paul O'Keeffe's *Some Sort of Genius, A Life of Wyndham Lewis,* a noisy, talented writer/painter; Robert Liddell's life of that lonely truth-telling poet of Alexandria, *Cavafy;* and David Gilmour's very moving work on Rudyard Kipling, *The Long Recesssional* (the book is moving partly because of the attention it brings to Kipling's everlasting sorrowing over his only son, John, who was killed on his very first day in the trenches of the Great War; Kipling spent years hunting the cemeteries of that war for John's resting-place, never found it; hard to read, those pages.). Kipling also has good counsel for writers: in his mature work, Gilmour writes of him, he obsessively excised superfluous words, said things like, "Wordiness is unforgiveable", and added, to his friend Edmund Gosse, that unnecessary words were "the enemy of vigour". He had learned this word-economy, he was fond of saying, in a youthful job as a telegraphist.

And, just in, there's Graham Robb's wonderfully enthusiastic *Balzac, A Biography*, a book in which Robb shows himself to much more advantage in this genre of writing than he was in his *Victor Hugo,* and one which persuades me, inexcusably late in life, that there can never have been a more inexhaustibly gifted or, no less memorably, *likeable* spirit among writers than Balzac. Of course there's Flaubert's famous and edgy line on him: "What a man he would have been had he known how to write!", but when you look at that sentence for a careful minute, and even though you know quite well what Flaubert *meant* by it, you can see his problem in constructing it: what Balzac was that was special, the sole reason we know of him, is that he was, almost ceaselessly, *a writer,* and "man" in that quoted sentence is just a blur, an obligatory sound to start things off, a failed noun by Flaubert's unique standards. What I would rather leave you with here is this anecdote, which emanates from the months near the end of Balzac's life when he was living with his lover Countess Eveline Hanska on her estate in the Ukraine. A valet on the estate wrote this about him: "You could see that he was very intelligent—far more intelligent even than those French tutors our neighbours send for from abroad to educate their children, for only a very wise man is so considerate towards poor people and servants." I'm very sure that that's a sentence to be moved by: there's its transparent authenticity (nothing writerly or practiced about it), and there's its charm (the valet saying of Balzac that he is far more intelligent "even than those French tutors", the certainty of this pronouncement, the sweep of the "far more" —you get a clear sense of a paying-off of old scores, of little hierarchy-based insults). Finally, perhaps, one warms to it because of the lovely Biblical thought about this famous and very wise man from a far-off land who is so "considerate" towards poor people and servants. Among whom, valets.

Last two. George D. Painter's *Marcel Proust,* which needs no comment from me; and Frank McLynn's *Robert Louis Stevenson,* which is much less well-known but is called "magnificent" on its back cover by Anthony Burgess. *Treasure Island* is a story I could still tell without missing any major episode, and I used, long ago, to worry my younger brother at night by singing Billy Bones's sea-chanties or doing my 'blind Pew' limping routine in our shared bedroom. Pew's "black spot" eventually worried even me, and I remember consciously dropping it from my repertoire. Stevenson was a much more remarkable man than I'd any idea of until I read McLynn's book Likeable, too: no competition for Balzac, but who was? Or is?

And one more paragraph, one which in a way doesn't belong here, since I have really nothing to say about the book it's to be found in. It's here, a late addition, simply because I can't keep it out, I think these are the most moving words from a husband about his wife I have ever read. "She has been", Charles Darwin wrote, of his wife Emma, "my greatest blessing, and I can declare that in my whole life I have never heard her utter one word which I would rather had been unsaid. I do not believe she has ever missed an opportunity of doing a kind action to anyone near her." *

---

*Darwin wrote these words in his autobiography, which was addressed to his sons. Emma (her biographer, Edna Healey, tells us) didn't allow the paragraph to be published in her lifetime.

On Translations

A FUNNY OLD THING, translations. They're as essential as anything to a good reader, without them where would we be, we'd be in a desert without water, we'd be holed up in our imagination-deprived houses the whole bleak winter without Tolstoy or Chekhov or Akhmatova or Mandelstam (if we couldn't read Russian), without Stendhal or Camus or Flaubert or Rimbaud (if…French), without Thomas Mann or Rilke or Robert Musil or Goethe (if…German), and so on. If for centuries we have had communication problems with other language-groups in spite of being able (as for a long while we have been able) to understand, thanks to translators and translations, their written signals, how much worse off would we have been without all those re-made, made accessible to us, books? It doesn't bear thinking about.

So, thank Whoever, for translations. Even if they're not as good, those foreign books in English tailoring, as they are in their own odd-looking clothes, at least they get through to us, we've learned to love them, and we tend to forget that there's anything at all suspect about what's going on when we read them. Which, though, in a way, there *is*. Something suspect, I mean. These words, these sentences, sounds, rhythms, rhymes, that someone else has substituted for what was originally there, for what's *Ur*, for what some Russian or German or French writer once made and what everything—everything!—except the narrative aspect of that which those writers originally made has been altered and is now being consumed by us amid a sort of music (those above-mentioned sounds, rhythms, etc) that the real author had nothing to do with and cannot judge, and maybe has never even looked at: this is, whether we talk about it a lot or not, in a sense sus-pect. And what's suspect is *the quality of the reading-experience*.

Which is not, as I think I've implied, to say that there's anything to be done about this. Translations exist that are in the opinion of many knowledgeable readers just about perfect, and translations also exist which many such readers think are a mockery, an involuntary parody of the original. What I plan to do here is to point to an instance or two where I think I can judge the quality of a translation, and offer some thoughts about this, about the sometimes-weirdness of it; and also to let you know how I once went about this myself. Translating, that is. On a modest scale, let me say: I translated a writer whom I admire a great deal but who wouldn't class himself among the reverberating names listed above, i.e., I haven't gotten around to translating *War and Peace*—I'd rather leave books like that to their own gigantic imitations of, well, war and peace.

Some thoughts initially about a few German works, German being neither my first nor my second language but a language I can read easily and speak half-decently. And it happens that the works I've paid most attention to in German are the poems of Rainer Maria Rilke and the novels and stories of Thomas Mann. Rilke I would attempt to translate (as a celebrated Canadian author once said to me when I asked her if she would give a reading at my university) "only if I were drugged and paid in gold". And no, not even then. Rilke may be the finest European poet of the 20th century (a dead heat with Yeats and Mandelstam, I think) but translating him—? You would have to sacrifice to the gods, and the libations, those on-your-knees proffered bowls, had better hold your own blood if you want to get near him, if you want to approach his words with your words; and that's not mere poetasterish babble, it really would be a near-lifetime dedication. Rilke not only managed (on many, many pages of his work) world-opening metaphors, similes of a grandeur that are almost always identifiably *his* in their persuasiveness, i.e., in their truth-to-the-occasion, also in their blazing newness, also in their voice, their sound, which in its quiet gravity hardly ever strays into ordinariness; —not only all that, but (to end the paragraph in what may seem a dwindling way) his poems very often rhyme.

Rhyme? I'm thinking now, I'm thinking it all the time on this page, of what's involved in translating this man—and rhyme, although it is only one of the problems (and opportunities!) in translating Rilke, is a central one. Because maybe, *maybe*, you can imagine the translator getting this or that Rilkean metaphor pretty well steered into position in its new (Englished) stanza; *maybe* a Rilkean simile can be approximately reproduced, a noun can be found that will relate, soundwise and sensewise, to its opposing noun (just before or just after the demanding, the inexorable 'like') in a way that's as pleasing or melodic or unexpected or shocking as the German original; *maybe*, too, the series of English words that you find to replace the forsaken, left behind there somewhere, series of German words, will seem to your reader to be shadowed by other English words that hover close and subtly affect you as you read, in the same way that word-shadows assist and accompany and add shape to those original Rilke-chosen German words. *Maybe* all these things can be managed (I don't for a second believe that they can, but I'm in reasonable spate here, so please just read on), but—here's the killer, the last of several riskily added-on straws—in rhyme? In a regular-format *abab* or *aabb* or *abcabc* or no regular rhyme at all but nevertheless rhyme, somewhere, doing its unnoticeable but pleasing, persuading, hypnotic, attention-enforcing job?

Well, enough, *basta*. It's never been done, people. Nobody's fault, really, it can't be done. There are a half-dozen fairly recent Rilke-translations visible in, as they say, all good bookshops, most of which latter are in distant towns by the way, but ne'mind. These translations exist and some are admirable, i.e. a decent poem albeit a different poem arises from its Rilkean model; and some are risible, a bad joke, a disservice to literature. But none do all the things that a Rilke poem, just lying mutely on its page for almost a hundred years by now, quietly does.

A few examples might disarm anyone who's beginning to think I exaggerate.

Here's a poem than which no Rilke-lyric has been translated more often; well, maybe *The Panther* has, but I think nothing else. It's called *Archäischer Torso Apollos*, and there's no problem translating the title: *Archaic Torso of Apollo*. After that, however, problems.

I'm going to take you through one stanza of this poem, the first stanza, i.e. the poem's first four lines, and compare these (narrowly, concentrating on rhyme to the near-exclusion of other and equally substantial areas of interest) to three different English-language translations. Centring on rhyme because all three of the translators have chosen to adopt Rilke's rhyme-pattern (abba) which helps to make this a quick study, it's a simple initial way to begin noticing problems and solutions, failures and successes, in translating. (Not that there's anything 'simple' about rhyme. If that search for the rhyming sound to end your line with, that clink that locks the rhyme in, isn't a true search, i.e. if it doesn't send the shaft down to the deepest level this poem you're working on can live at, deeper than you could have reached *without* this self-imposed rhyme-search, then you stopped digging too soon, you accepted a word merely because it rhymed, it simply slid into place without making anything new happen; and if this occurs even twice, no, even once, your poem's probably already dead in the water, it's already, *flottaison blême et ravie**, lost to human sight.)

So, this stanza. Rilke's first line is *Wir kannten nicht sein unerhörtes Haupt*. Translating this line you could start off with, piece of cake, "Well, the English for this is *We didn't know his*—" —but then you'd grind to a halt. You'd know that the last word in the line is 'head', that's easy enough—but you only get to 'head' by going through *unerhörtes*, a word which, unluckily for you as translator, means, potentially, several quite distinct things, and it means or implies all of them at once. It means, yes, unheard-of, but not quite that, it's much more resonant in the German and more ambiguous too; it also means, at times, unacceptable, unbelievable (in the way we say 'unbelievable' of some awful event); and in its closeness to '*hören*' (to hear), it suggests that this hasn't been heard, hasn't ever even been spoken of before. It's a loaded word, that is; as loaded as any word you'll ever have to meet head-on like this. It's rich in its suggestiveness, in the fact that small echoes and eddies of all these meanings are present in this three-and-a-half-syllable word, and they can't be elucidated let alone absorbed *separately*; and the problem it sets before the translator is, how to come close to this coiled power in this first line, all of it tensely present in this one word, without making elaborate detours in an effort not to lose any of those echoes and eddies.

One of the versions I have on my desk, this one's by Vernon Watkins, caves in right away, with "We did not know his unfamiliar head". Unfamiliar? There's a friendly solution to the problem, *mein Gott*, it's even tautological now, this opening line: not only is this head 'unfamiliar', but "we did not know" it before. Bad stuff. Here's C.F.MacIntyre: "Never will we know his fabulous head...". There's a needless shift from present to future tense here but at least McIntyre doesn't domesticate Apollo as the god was domesticated in that first-

---

*From Arthur Rimbaud's possibly world-best poem "Le Bateau Ivre".

quoted version: 'fabulous', though, is an easy sort of clutch at significance, a balloon of an adjective, it's far, far short of the use Rilke has made of *unerhörtes*. Thirdly, from a very good *Selected Poetry of Rainer Maria Rilke* by Stephen Mitchell: "We cannot know his legendary head". The "cannot" here isn't Rilke's idea which is, as in Watkins's version, "did not"; one might be inclined to guess, *im voraus* as it were, that "cannot" would be more powerful and hence a permitted change here, as if everything's a plus as long as it brings a power-surge along with it, but on reflection, *no*, short-lived power-add-on or not I think it's the sort of weight-shift inside the line that a translator needs to be chary of, needs to look very hard at; needs to be suspicious, if needs be, of his own ambitions inside this poem that is very far from entirely his. Aside from that, though, the Mitchell version of this poem seems in general to me superior to most, he's done some lovely things further down the page; but since I'm not planning to go much further down the page just now, all I'll say about "legendary" here is that it's neck-and-neck with "fabulous", both of them in their frilly Agamemnon mini-costumes staring longingly at the disappearing form of *unerhörtes* far ahead.

So, that's a central issue in translations: the fact that, very often, a word in all its subtleties cannot be duplicated in another language. Naturally one doesn't, can't, shouldn't hope for or argue for exact facsimiles. What one can look for, though, is a poem that works on its own and that reflects, as closely as is manageable, the tone, the degree of clarity (accessibility), and the narrative content (imagery, continuity) of the original. In my experience the spectrum of techniques adopted by translators is…endless, it arches from horizon to horizon. There exist translations in which almost all of the images of the original poem have vanished, but the stanza-form, rhyme-scheme, and, let's say, the noise-level of that original are reproduced almost ostentatiously, triumphantly. There are also translations, many of them (Stephen Spender did a number of these, Rilke among them), which are confessedly written by someone, usually some known poet, who neither speaks nor reads the poem's original language, and who does his 'translation' with the aid of a very literal prose version of the original, this prose version supplied by a native speaker of that original language. The poet-translator in such cases, working from that prose version supplied by an uncredentialed whoever, hasn't a clue about or a morsel of reverence for the rhythms of the original, or for its place in its own literature, or for the familiarity or otherwise of expressions used in that poem on its home ground (e.g. is this phrase very familiar in its own culture? is it perhaps even a cliché, perhaps knowingly, cynically employed here? if it is, then you must try to find a similarly clichéd expression in your translation; or is it , instead, in its native habitat, very fresh, pulsing with new energies that its readers can only be astonished by? if so, let's see how well you cope with astonishment*).

You will understand that I'm not impressed by persons who call themselves translators and who operate on this sort of basis; who work, that is, from a prose version supplied by a native (Russian, French, etc) speaker.

As promised, I'm not going to take you through all of the 'Archaic Apollo', short though it be. But, continuing with our first stanza, Rilke's second line is, "*darin die Augenäpfel reiften. Aber*". The prose version (for any Stephen Spenders who are casting an indolent but acquisitive eye on this) would be, easy-peasy, "in which (wherein) the eye-apples ripened. But". What do our three translators do with this? Watkins: "Where hung the ripening apples of his eyes". MacIntyre: "where the eyes' apples slowly ripened. Yet". Mitchell: "with eyes like ripening fruit. And yet his torso".

OK, so there's nothing as insurmountable as *unerhörtes* in this second line of the stanza, but there are a few of the typical problems a translator faces. The three solutions, as you see, vary. Watkins introduces "hung" where no hanging is to be seen in Rilke's line, or anywhere else in his poem; not a criminal act, although it's not really helpful with regard to 'eyes'. Maybe he was forced towards it because he'd decided to use 'eyes' as one of the two line-ending rhymes of his stanza (he makes a real dog's breakfast out of his third line, where his

---

*I can't let pass here a line from a letter Rilke wrote on February 1, 1914, to a friend named Magda von Hattingberg. He's not writing about the missing head of his archaic Apollo, he's writing about the head of the Sphinx. He's writing from Egypt and he's just seen the Sphinx for the first time. He writes, "...I reproached myself for not experiencing this deeply enough; wasn't it necessary to reach places in my astonishment where I had never been before?"

rhyme with 'eyes' will appear, but that's for my next paragraph), and maybe he felt he needed an extra event in order to pad out the length of the line; if you try to redesign his line (let's see now, "Where were the ripening…" …erm, no, doesn't work. "Where the ripening apples of his eyes were"? No again, because if he replaces 'eyes' with 'were' here, he'll have to find a new rhyming word in line 4). For some reason Watkins also capitalizes the first word of every line in the poem: I've no idea why he would do this, since Rilke capitalizes only the first word in every sentence (i.e. 'sentence' not 'line'). MacIntyre has "where the eyes' apples slowly ripened. Yet". He's got his apples "slowly" ripening, where Rilke allows his reader to decide what degree of haste is involved; and he's chosen, as you'll have noticed, a different rhyme-word; now the rhyme-setting word isn't Watkins's 'eyes', it's "yet", which gives MacIntyre a terrific palette of choice. As for Mitchell, he has : "with eyes like ripening fruit. And yet his torso". Again, a different rhyme (Mitchell will make good use of this in line 4); this is altogether a much better line, seems to me, than either of the others; you can see those eyes coming into a sort of life; so here is a translator doing what only the very best at the craft can do, which is to make a line that doesn't deviate radically from the poem's imagery, but manages a really fresh jolt of energy that is all its own.

Third lines: "*sein torso glühte noch wie ein Kandelaber*": prose version, "his torso still glows like a candelabra". This is where Watkins loses the plot totally: "But still his torso candelabra-wise". Yes, adding that hyphenated 'wise' means he's got his rhyme for 'eyes', but… 'nuff said. MacIntyre: "his torso glows: a candelabrum set". Ouch. 'Candelabrum' does neither line nor torso-image any favours, the 'brum' of that last syllable is far too thumpy. Mitchell: "is still suffused with brilliance from inside,"—not bad, I'd say, but it *forces* us, his readers, or tries to, by telling us about this "brilliance", where Rilke relies on his candelabra-simile all on its own, he invites us to see the 'brilliance' ourselves, he creates brilliance instead of naming it. 'Brilliance' is, anyway, one of those descriptive terms which through over-use has just about lost whatever power it once possessed. The three solutions, as you see, vary, to say no more.

And now the 4th and last line: "*in dem sein Schauen, nur zurückgeschraubt*". The prose version here would be, "in which his gaze (literally, his "looking"), only wound back" ('wound' in the sense of 'screwed'; but the latter has some baggage in English which I understand it does not have in German—baggage which the translator must take note of). Watkins: "Glows, where his gazing, screwed back from the dead,"....well, I told you he'd lost the plot. MacIntyre: "before his gaze which is pushed back and hid". Mitchell: "like a lamp, in which his gaze, now turned to low,". Both MacIntyre and Mitchell recognize the problem with 'screwed' and take evasive action; neither of them appears to have considered my very-recent suggestion of 'wound' as a one-word one-syllable substitute ('geschraubt' is of course two syllables, but anyway), which hurts my feelings but not much. Mitchell's evasive act seems to me pretty successful: "turned to low" does, once again, as this translator did with "ripening fruit", energize the scene, it allows us to judge how the scene now looks, it's new, for God's sake, in the context of a look, of a gaze, of eyes.

I realize that I'm doing no favours to any of the four poets by setting the lines before you in this mutilated form, but with a little effort you can, if you like, reconstitute the three translated versions and Rilke's original stanza. My aim was not really to award points, although I've done a bit of that, but only to give an example of what the preceding paragraphs of this piece were on about: namely, the complex and endlessly subtle but also the very practical difficulties facing a translator, in this case a translator of one of the recently-ended century's finest poets.

Prose, now, is a different matter. Words are of more individual value in a 12-line lyric poem than they are in a thousand-page novel. This does not, however, mean that a novel's translator should feel licenced to roam about freely on her or his own, adding and sub-tracting words or images with either straight or gay abandon; although some of them, where I can judge, behave so. One of my favourite Thomas Mann novellas, *Tonio Kröger* (Mann always said it was among his favourite works, and the closest thing he'd ever done to straight autobiography), begins with his protagonist, Tonio, coming out of school along with his friend Hans Hansen, and the second paragraph mentions how the boys pull their caps off "in awe before the Olympian hat and ambrosial beard of a master moving homewards with measured stride...." Well, Mann's actual description of the appearance of that schoolmaster, of his hat and his beard, translated as directly as it may and can be, is that the former is a "Wotan-hat", and the latter a 'Jupiter-beard'. Why the switch to 'Olympian' and 'ambrosial', is what I ask myself. Doesn't the translator trust us to have heard of Wotan? Or does he think 'Olympian' more majestic? Or…? To me the change here is from the specific to the general, which may not always be a bad idea but, by and large, *is*. 'Ambrosial' is straight-up irritating: 'Jupiter' is no sweetiepie, whereas 'ambrosial' suggests something studied, in this context maybe even dyed, soft vapours envelope it; "divinely fragrant", the OED pronounces.

Another example. In *Death in Venice*, also a novella and one often published along with the Tonio, Mann's final description of his protagonist, Gustav von Aschenbach, who has just died while sitting in his beach-chair on the Lido in Venice, tells us that he lies (and this is my literal translation from the German) 'sideways and sunk down in his chair'. The most widely available published translation of this death-scene, by H.T. Lowe-Porter, omits anything resembling 'sideways' and gives us only "the elderly man sitting there collapsed in his chair". Admitting that the German language permits Mann to avoid any noun like 'man' and that a translator will probably have to use that word or something very like it, still, 'elderly' is just not permissible here: we know Aschenbach's age very well already, the story has indeed focused to a large extent on this, and in the context of Mann's delicate language-manoeuvrings 'elderly' is crass. Ditto 'collapsed': 'collapsed' can give us the impression of a shambles, a sprawl: it fails altogether to lead us towards the very clear image Mann has given us, the specific posture, the 'sideways' Aschenbach 'sunk down in' his chair.

These are puzzling matters which extend far beyond Thomas Mann. My guess is that this sort of slovenliness (combined with sheer incapacity) is/was pandemic at the turn of the 19th-20th centuries. At the end of a minutely developed and moving novella called *Un Coeur simple* Gustave Flaubert is describing the death of 'a simple heart', a serving-maid named Félicité who has grown old in the service of an uncaring woman in a French village, and whose only cherished companion throughout most of her life has been a parrot, whose body at death the serving-woman has had stuffed and kept in its cage in her tiny room. The novella ends with the servant's death, a scene which

Flaubert describes with consummate delicacy; with, I will say, love. I've described it as 'moving' because it's the only time in the entire novella that 'love' has been shown to this woman, except by the author, except by the unwavering attentiveness Flaubert has brought to her otherwise scorned existence. And this love is shown very especially in the story's last long sentence, not via any direct claim or pronouncement (of love) made by this author, but by the beautifully managed language with which he describes that death. What Flaubert gives us, having described Félicité's closing her eyes, having described the slowing beats ("movements", he writes) of her heart, is this: "…and ,as she exhaled her last breath, she thought she saw, in the opening skies, a gigantic parrot, soaring above her head".

And what does the translation have here, in place of "soaring"? It has "fluttering".

Well, I feel no one should be forced to continue past the *grotes-querie* of that 'translation' without first taking a turn in the garden, a few deep breaths, anything to dislodge the feelings that language-misuse of this order must arouse. Flaubert's own word here, by the way, is *'planant'*. I've suggested 'soaring', or it could be just 'soar', neither of which satisfies me totally: we just don't have the equivalent of , or in this specific case anything as good as the French verb *'planer'*, which oddly enough works not badly to an English ear and eye as long as we *don't* translate it. It works not badly partly because we do have *planes*, meaning either *levels* of a sort or *aircraft*, and with both those background shadings at work it then conceivably achieves a degree of rightness which might even surpass the effect a French reader gets from it…but this is becoming tortuous, I'm out of here.

Point is, even a superficial look into this business, the business of literary translation, can lead to the conviction that the first translators to arrive on the scene and feast on the great 19th and 20th century European novelists were given *carte blanche* by their perhaps-intimidated reviewers. The works themselves, one can feel (*Anna Karenina, Madame Bovary, Der Zauberberg*) were so exhilaratingly powerful that to complain (and how many of the established critics and reviewers of the time knew the original languages of these *Meisterwerke* anyway?) must have seemed graceless as well as ungrateful; and, granted the forbidding enormity of the task, *Anna*'s 800 pages,

W&P's 1350 pages, it's understandable that those first translators held the field for aeons, for most of a century, before anyone else came along with the stamina to challenge them, to provide better versions or at least a choice of versions. Of late this has happened in some cases, i.e. new and better translations have appeared (Proust comes to mind); I could wish that Nabokov, who did his beloved Pushkin, had lived another fifty years and done Tolstoy and Turgenev and Chekhov. Who knows, if he had, what pages would have come into even more fiery or lambent life than we presently know them to have?

In near-conclusion: a recent *Guardian* piece approvingly quotes Miguel de Cervantes's description of the reading of a translation as "looking at the Flanders tapestries from the wrong side". You can, Cervantes went on, "see the basic shapes but they are so filled with threads that you cannot fathom their original lustre". It's an imagination-rich comparison, which is why I'm happy to repeat it here, but in its largely negative message it strikes me as self-disqualifying: though bits of lustre may have fallen off it here and there in its long journey from Cervantes's 17th-century Spanish to current English, there's plenty left for us glowing in these tapestry-threads, seems to me, and neither *The Guardian*, probably, nor you, probably, nor I, certainly, would have fathomed any of it without a succession of translators having gotten among them.

I've come to the final stage of this piece, which is where I reminisce a bit about my own experience as a translator. During the several years of my stay in Stockholm, I'd been introduced to the poetry of Tomas Tranströmer, and had come to regard him as one of the finest living poets not only of Sweden but of *hela världen* (as you might have guessed, 'the whole world'). Years later, back in Canada, and having sampled the available translations of TT's work into English (some of these by American poets, Robert Bly among these, but the foremost being Robin Fulton, a Scot who lives in Norway) I came across a very recent book of Tranströmer's (in Swedish) and, thinking I could do better with certain of his poems than one or two of his translators had done, I wrote to him to ask if I might take this new book of his on with the intention (if he approved of the end-product, and if I could then interest a Canadian publisher in it) of publishing it in Canada. Tomas, as I was soon invited to call him, and his wife

Monica, who looked after the correspondence (Tomas had suffered a stroke which inhibited the physical side of writing/typing), approved, and off we went.

Well, off *I* went.

There was a misunderstanding from the beginning, I have to say. I thought the book (called *För Levande och Döda*; 'For the living and the dead') had not yet been translated into English. This was not the case. The poems had appeared in the U.S. one year before my versions (Buschekbooks 1996) would appear ; a U.K.translation came along a year after mine. All I'll say about this is that it was a true misunderstanding, not really caused by language difficulties (most of the letters, except for phrases here and there, which I wrote to the Tranströmers were in English; Monica replied in Swedish; this caused neither of us any problems). The Tranströmers assumed I knew about the U.S.book, and never mentioned the fact of that book to me; I assumed that our correspondence concerned a first-time translation, and never asked if this was so. I mention it only to make clear that I had not read any Englishing of the poems before going to work on them. I still hadn't read that other version when my book appeared.

And what did I feel when I did read those other versions? Nothing very earthshaking: I felt that some of those other translators' lines were superior to mine, and some not so, some inferior. I had been a reader of Tomas's work for some decades, ever since I came upon his first books in Scandinavia in the late fifties and early sixties; I thought he was as good as any living European poet, as time passed I became convinced he ought to be a Nobelist; if Heaney deserved that award, and maybe he did, then Tranströmer deserved it equally; deserved it a shade more, is what I, to be honest, thought. And still think. What this meant was that translating him was a task, an enterprise, the worth of which I didn't ever question. It's not a simple encounter, translating an entire book of poems, it's not a chore to undertake unless you feel, all the while, that you're dealing with an imagination you admire, unless you feel that you're living in close communion with a sensibility that you feel *lifted* by, *moved* by. In other words unless there's something in it for *you*. And if this feeling only grows stronger as the days and weeks of finding, of trying to find, a rhythm and a form and a language-level that will communicate to English-speaking readers something close to what's on that Swedish page, those 25-odd Swedish pages, then this is time well spent. It's a special feeling. I had it all the time I was working on *For Levande och Döden* and I have it still.

An example of what we Tranströmer-translators got up to. The first poem in Tomas's book was called *Den Bortglömde Kaptenen*. The literal translation here would be 'The Away-Forgotten Captain'; both Robin Fulton and I ducked, just a bit, I think, and rendered it as 'The Long-Forgotten Captain'. Fact is, the captain *does* die 'away', he dies in wartime in a Cardiff hospital after his ship was torpedoed; the Swedish usage, *bortglömde*, was there and Tranströmer used it, why shouldn't he. I felt, though, that to follow him literally would draw too much attention to the title, would be exotic where the Swedish was not, hence 'long' replaces 'away'. A loss, though, even if an insignificant one.

That stanza starts like this, in the Fulton version. "We have many shadows. I was walking home/ in the September night when Y/ climbed up out of his grave after forty years/ and kept me company..." Mine was the same except that "bobbed" replaced "climbed". Fulton could with absolute justice point out that the captain died on dry land, hence no 'bobbing' was involved in his last moments. I liked "bobbed" because of the ship's having gone down at sea, I thought the word unexpected and not irrelevantly unexpected; I thought that there was more going on, more action in that line, with 'bobbed'.

Here's another such comparison. My reason, by the way, for these comparisons is not in order to show my continuous triumphings (which, not incidentally, isn't the case—if nobody was looking I might well have appropriated some of Fulton's solutions in preference to mine); it's only to show the sorts of freedom a translator has, the creative aspect, the choices to be made. The poem goes on, very powerfully, to evoke the convoy, the frailty of the ship out on that hostile ocean, we're invited to visualize it. It puts this scene in the past tense so that it becomes a matter of how we "saw war's ocean" (Fulton); or, (Coles) "saw the war's sea". From one point of view I like Fulton's 'ocean' better here than my 'sea', it's broader, vaster; on the other hand, Tranströmer's word here is "*hav*", a very short word, you'll notice, one syllable and three letters...a little like 'sea', come to think of it.

Can't leave this without one more comparison. There's a line in the poem which I translated as "It was an inward cry that bled him to death…". Fulton: "It was an internal weeping that bled him to death". Obvious win for this latter version: it has the *process* of bleeding which 'cry' does not.

I could go on at length here but will not. In recent years Tomas Tranströmer has been writing almost exclusively haiku , and I've tried my hand at some of these, mostly, I'm glad to be able to say, to the Tranströmers' approval. Once or twice, also, we've had some amicable back-and-forths about a line or a word, once I recall Monica felt I'd gotten away from the Tranströmer voice while Tomas felt that regardless of voice I had made a good poem out of it which made it OK by him. It's all, though, been a pleasure from my point of view. And what I've learned here, aside from anything I've mentioned so far in this little essay, is that the sort of intimate and lengthy relationship that translation involves you in *can* mean that what you admire most in the work of this man or woman you're translating reappears, in fitful gleams and glimpses, in your own work—and that's nothing short of, yes, wonderful. Tomas, in the poems of his I admire most, has a simplicity which just takes my breath away, it's a naked undecorated stripped-down-ness which I think, now, after this long face-to-face, I'd recognize anywhere, in any anthology of no-names-no-pack-drills modern poetry from any corner of the universe. If I show even fragmentary, even sporadic signs of this in anything I may write in what's left of life, *good*.

A Sentimental Education

Growing Up in Woodstock,
Toronto, London, Stockholm,
Florence

[Another dedication]

To all those known or merely glimpsed here, in your youth and, yes, more than once in a while, beauty, now grown old (and finding this just as unforeseen as I am finding it), greetings, and, here and there, like then, love

1.

RISKY TITLE. On the one hand, Flaubertian, an impossible act to follow. On the other, too suitable to sidestep, too exactly what I feel when I take my long look back. What I mean to do with it is this: I mean to show how an individual's growth—whatever we call that myriad of felt, seldom-documented experiences that, beginning in earliest childhood, forms itself in him or her—can, if actively pursued and cultivated, lead to a relatively consistent series of attitudes and judgments, of values 'aesthetic' in nature but also operative politically, socially, in one's public life as well as one's kept-to-oneself thoughts.

Well, no, that's *not* what I mean to show. Really not. Too diffuse, too unhorizoned. That way lies madness, lies an endless and Byzantine discourse, lies Matthew Arnold. I have a more modest chase in view. Namely or chiefly: myself. The self I hardly noticed while I was growing and changing inside the body that carried me about. Hardly anybody *does* do that, is my belief. Really notice, I mean. Sounds from outside are forever preempting or blurring those early, frail, softly-surrendered murmurs of self, of who one might be becoming, a being shaping itself even while it's resisting and mistrusting many of the signs of that shaping. Proust, who surely recorded more of these murmurs than any other human being and paid the price by having so few wholly-signed-on, signed-on-for-the-full-ride readers (though more lingeringly loved, I will suppose, by those few than any other writer) nails a main cause of this indifference to the early self by speaking of it as "an instrument which the uniformity of habit has rendered silent"—one of those many, many lines which instruct one to forgive the thin embroideries of the preceding ten paragraphs of his book. He says something else about this too, veering as he does so into an adjoining territory which is probably a little too beautiful for me to do much more with than glance at it in swift passing. Explaining, perhaps, why people of my considerable years find themselves thinking more than they formerly did about their beginnings, he writes (in *The Captive*, which I happened to be reading during a late edit of this book), "When we have passed a certain age, the soul of the child we were and the souls of the dead from whom we have sprung come to lavish on us their riches and their spells." Have you read a more mind-ambushing sentence than that anywhere lately? In any case, these are the sorts of things I have looked at, looked at briefly, at first, and then lengthily, in persuading myself not only where my focus, my various foci, should be—it and they should be on my first few decades—and also, in the name of both candour and clarity, hinting to me that I might do well to choose an exact year in which the investigation halts. Which I now do, choosing my end-of-decade 29th year. Up to that year I mean to trace, insofar as I can, my own developing sympathies and antipathies in matters pertaining, more or less, to the arts, but connecting with as many other aspects of my life as I can in brief space manage. And I hope to do this with a minimum of yolkhead flâneuring, in a spirit which will be broad enough, familiar enough to my readers, that it will at least seem to take its energy from generous impulses rather than elitist ones; impulses that invite the reader into an experiencing of recovered pleasures and a reawakening of once-pleasing, now and then *loved*, sights, voices, acts, all these returning from and in remembrance of, yes, lost time.

The Germans own the best single word for this. *Weltanschauung.* Way of looking at the world, way of feeling about things. And 'a sentimental education' or even the certifiably-dubious 'a matter of taste' are amorphous terms to run with, so let me short-cut them and simply say that I'm starting this section with a motley collection of names and faces—in particular, this first part, the faces of people who as I now scroll over my past look back at me more steadfastly than I, at the time, paid nearly enough attention to. In a way, and this is what I try to persuade myself of, those faces *haven't* gone, that's memory's great gift, and when I think like that then even those years of my inattention don't prevent me from recovering them, sometimes with a startling clarity. How often I sense their discreet presence, and can feel my "remorse at not having lived profoundly enough in the old house"!* After them come other faces and lives, these are the artists and writers, met and un-met, mostly unmet; and accompanying them

---

*From Gaston Bachelard's *The Poetics of Space*

are the faces and lives that those artists and writers *made*. Gallery-walls in a dozen cities bear privately-honoured paintings, music-fragments reliably recur, and there's that critical armload of necessary, life-companioning books. All together these may move towards, they may cluster near, the phenomena of love.

A big word, the one at the end there.

2.

I BEGIN, UNAVOIDABLY, with my childhood. A home in a town called Woodstock in the centre of Western Ontario. A father, Jack Coles, whose bio beneath the photo in his university's graduation-book says he was "a man of few words" who went to college "to study something". Not untrue, the laconic bit, but he must have risen to a completed sentence now and then: he did, after all, find words to persuade Alice Brown, who won Victoria College's top award, the 'Senior Stick', to marry him. No popularity contest, that award, the Stick was straightup awarded to the best student in the college. One 'Stick' for the girls, as they were certainly called, and one for the men, as they were certainly called. The winning male in that graduating year of 1920 as recorded in *Torontonensis* was Douglas Bush, who went on to become Harvard's head of English and a world-renowned scholar. A group photo shows these two, Alice Brown and Douglas Bush. They are at opposite ends of the begowned group, and each is clutching her or his Stick.

My mother then went to Sackville Ladies' College in the Maritimes to teach History for a year before returning to Toronto where she and my father married before four witnesses, viz., his parents and brothers (her parents had both died before her third birthday). I think it's OK now, after, in Yeats's phrase, long silence (I only learned of what I'm about to tell you after my mother's death), to let a few people know that at her graduation three of her History profs at the U of T, led by George M.Wrong, the Department Chairman, banded together to offer her the equivalent of a three-year scholarship at Oxford: of a Rhodes, in fact (women weren't eligible in those years); she turned this down in favour of the above-mentioned solution. My father, an unusually fine athlete, had, prior to his marriage, gone to France in WWI and fought at Arras (because of the long-echoing, unifying effect of those two syllables, 'Arras', I like to think that Jack Coles, 2ndLt., East Ontario Regiment, may have glimpsed in passing, may have shared, for a moment, a duckboard over the terrible drowning mud, with Edward Thomas,2ndLt., Royal Artillery. Edward Thomas is for me, of all English poets, the one I turn to most often. He was killed by the blast of a shell in April, 1917, at that battle of

Arras, which was really the beginning of Passchendaele. He was exactly twenty years older than my father when one of them stood aside, as I like to think, for a courteous second, to allow the other to pass on that duckboard) .

> Now all roads lead to France
> And heavy is the tread
> Of the living; but the dead
> Returning lightly dance.*

Jack and Alice survived the Depression and had four children, of which I was the second.** Alice lived four years longer than she would have wanted to, those last four years with what was not then diagnosed as Alzheimers but seems now to be have been such. A few years later my father (who'd had a stroke and was warned they were coming to take him to hospital the next morning, an experience he'd vigorously evaded all his long life) turned his face to the wall during the night and triumphantly died. Good people. Better than that, but neither of them favoured hyperbole so I'll leave it there. No I won't. My father was as honest a human being as anyone I've known, and as generous, and never asked to what use one was putting his generosity, which

---

*From the poem 'Roads', by Edward Thomas

** In fact there was another son, born in that shy condition of his a year before I appeared, a stillborn would-be brother of whom I think a few times each year. One of the thoughts I then always have is that if he had lived I would probably not have come along at all, any plans for me would have been shelved, or, to put it less domestically, abandoned. And he would then not, of course, have merely gone about duplicating the life I have lived, no, his sounds and scenes would have been his own , they'd have started a year before my arrival and so all the events attendant upon them would have gone by during that year before I reached my own, later, sounds and scenes; reached them only to find them used up by him before I got there, exhausted of the vitality they once burgeoned with.

What would he have done with them, *in* them, his own sounds and scenes? I have once or twice thought: *he would have done all of the things which I wish I had done*. He would have become or reached all of those states (which would perhaps have been heights) which I have at times wished I could have become or reached. And then I think: You mean he would have become Tom Stopppard?

Tom Stoppard? Well, no... thoughts rush past, inflating at the same time as they dwindle....

is surely the crown of that quality. My mother was as intelligent and quiet-about-it ditto.* *Now* I'll leave it. My father bequeathed his physique with an unusual precision to me, although I didn't make as good use of it on tennis and basketball courts and his (now mine, soon my son's) Brunswick-Balke-Collender billiards table as he had. Maybe *half* as good use, though, which has always been OK by me. My mother?— *books,* what else, are what she bequeathed. In my early and middle teens I read my way through her library: all of Thomas Hardy, five vols. of Constance Holme (of whom you have not heard, though you could hear much worse: *Trumpet in the Dust, The Splendid Fairing, The Lonely Plough*), all of Willa Cather, all of what little there is of Winifred Holtby, some of Hugh Walpole (at one time considered an epigone of Henry James, never a compliment really, though nowadays he'd probably settle for it), and two soft-leather-bound collections of short stories, one of these Chekhov and the other Balzac. I also remember reading Franz Werfel's *The Forty Days of Musa Dagh* several times (it had a lengthy erotic passage in it, probably unnoticeably so by today's standards; took all my attention, though), and there were also a few odd choices of my own; e.g., from the local library, Oswald Spengler's *The Decline of the West.* (A taste I apparently shared with the young Northrop Frye, according to his biographer; a turgid book, as I remember, so it's hard to be sure why I persevered. It could be, though, that the absence of any other date-stamps at the back of the book spoke for it). Also lots of Zane Grey and almost as much of G.H. Henty. And *Chums Annuals* from my grandmother's attic, featuring the same square-jawed Hentyesque youths (though in print so fine only ten-year-olds could read it) repeatedly dying with Gordon in Khartoum or all alone in the Khyber Pass or much nearer home on the Plains of Abraham. Some of those years I kept an exact accounting of names, publishers, dates, always with a no-nonsense synopsis, as in *Russians Don't Surrender,* "raids, liaisons, corresp.later killed", *What Next, O Duce,* "B. Mussolini, blacksmith's son.", *Balisand,* "Richard Bale dies on way back in canoe", *Stalky and Co.,* "in India with Sikhs, Pathans"; *Dead Ned,* "Ned hung (*sic*) at Newgate", *Cavalcade of the English Novel,* (no comment).

---

* The 'ditto' refers to "as anyone I've known".

Steered clear of girls in H.S ., mostly due to a worry about being so tall—the NBA with its nowadays admired and very rich seven-footers had not happened yet and it was not cool to be the only 6' 4" kid in the building. Or so I thought. If it was even half-cool I didn't know it. Would've happily changed heights with Tiny Thompson, who was five foot and a bit and held court every day after school in The Hub, a teenager joint in the middle of town which I may have ventured cautiously into, oh, once. I knew that if I ventured there again everybody inside would instantly stop the chatter and just goggle upwards. In lieu of that, either alone or with a normal-length pal, I shot baskets in the school gym most days from four until the janitor shut things down. Really admired, however, the school's prettiest girl, ringletted brunette who usually came first on our class's report cards, and whom I took, just once, to a movie. I remember our long walk home from the Capitol Theatre on the icy sidewalks, past the lounging woo-hooing Zombies on the 'Y' steps, she mentioning a few times how slippery it was and me agreeing but not daring to offer her my hand. Poor sap.

List of words in a diary of my 14th year. Atrophy, culpable,chauvinist, alembic, hirsute, hegemony, nadir, Bacchus, *mutatis mutandis.*

Victoria College in the fall of '45 was full of returned vets, there were only a few of us teen-age freshmen in that First Year intake. Maybe a good thing, maybe not. Those outnumbered 18-year-old virgins got to learn a lot of brilliantly rhyming navy/air-force songs (*The Old Monk, It Was the Good Ship Venus,* and, my favourite, *The Persian Kitten*) which they wouldn't have run into in a regular-type year, but had a greatly reduced hope of winning awards, a Rhodes Scholarship, say, when it came time to graduate. My parents had been college friends of Lester Pearson and his wife Marion, I'd heard of his Rhodes more than once and had been aiming in that general direction since I was about 12. At that age I wrote to the Rhodes committee for information and was thanked for my interest but advised to try them again at some later date, i.e., to cool it. When the time arrived I duly applied and made it to the last call, the final five. The winner was an outstanding student and fine man who'd been taken prisoner at Hong Kong and spent the war in a Japanese prison camp and had got a major decoration, probably not a VC but close. He was absolutely the right choice among the five of us, three of whom were also vets, so this is no whinge, it's only…a small whinge. In a normal year I'd have been off to Oxford the next September.* Well, that's always been my opinion, shared (I should add) by no one.

Northrop Frye and Marshall McLuhan may have been the two finest teachers available on any university campus in the world during my undergraduate years in Toronto and I had courses with both, five with Frye. Also one course with E.J.Pratt, Canada's then most celebrated poet, celebrated also for his absentmindedness, who in my first year gave me an unusually high mark on a Shakespeare exam. Meeting me on Vic's steps one snowy day he shook my hand, told me I was "the best", and walked on, waving. He then stopped and called back, for emphasis, "The best, Harris!"

I spent two of my undergrad summers at Trois-Pistoles in Quebec, and acquired a not-bad French accent. In the school's tennis finals I lost to the local curé who, in conformity with the inflexible dress-code of those times, wore his cassock and large-brimmed black hat throughout our three sets on a boiling clay court. He was ambidextrous, which of course meant he had no backhand: this I felt almost made up to him for the handicap of the Hallowe'en gear. My best T-P friend was a lovely Haitian guy of about my own size, named Lucien Thébaud, who arrived with a half-dozen cream-coloured linen suits, one of which he always insisted I borrow whenever we went out on the village. He was studying at the U. of Montreal but had determined to leave before his sophomore year began, full of indignation that the University Library had refused him access to the works of the 'godless' Jean-Jacques Rousseau. I always thought that Lucien, so smart, so handsome, so sweet, would sooner or later surface as Prime Minister down there on his island, but maybe Duvalier (called 'Papa Doc' which sounds like an endearment, but there was nothing endearing about that butcher) felt the same way about him and took steps to preempt

---

*List of prodigious Rhodes-type achievements on request.

It happens that while completing this section with its mention of the exceptional nature of the competition that year, I was rereading Evelyn Waugh's *Brideshead Revisited*. Here's a sentence from that novel's early pages: "My father in his youth sat for All Souls and, in a year of hot competition, failed…" Hot competition. Guys never forget things like that.

any surfacing.

How many people whom one knew back in those invulnerable days have turned out to be…not invulnerable!

Back in Toronto I wrote for *The Varsity*, a daily in those years; Sports Editor one year (at $5 a week, enough for two or three meals out), columnist the next. Hugh Kenner, later to become the world's leading Ezra Pound expert, was Editor-in-Chief one of those years, a very tall, etiolated man who wrote his editorials in seclusion, already signing on with a singular crew. One of the most stunning women I've ever seen (right up there with a blonde Lübeckerin called Heidi, who doesn't make the cut into this narrative, having arrived in my life *after* my 29th year to heaven) I met while playing a drop-in game of bridge in U.C.'s Common Room. She pulled up a chair beside either me or South with her beautiful supermodel's face and her skinny body, black hair tight to her small perfect head. Today she'd be jetting off to the catwalks of Rome, Tokyo, London and making lots. No idea how our very brief connection ended. No idea what she said, ever, what she was doing in U.C. (she wasn't a student) that day, nothing, not a sound or a word survives. Anne D'Arcand, I hope you didn't spend all that beauty on the indifferent air. On some *lumpen* horse's ass, I of course mean.

Went to Europe in the summer before my last undergraduate year, on a Dutch boat, the *S.S .Tabinta*. A friend and I took bicycles with us, intending to cycle from Rotterdam to Paris. All those Dutch cyclists training for the Tour de France, zipping past us on the narrow cycle-paths! If your front wheel wavered there'd be a pile-up. Nobody's wheel wavered. At a street-corner in Rotterdam, waiting among the Stuka-flattened buildings for the light to change, a Dutch kid of about our age, leaning on his handlebars and looking across at us as we leaned on ours, invited us to his home for dinner and a place to spend the night. Klaus was his name. Sometimes I know his surname too, but—ah, here it comes, out of the almost sixty-years-old shadows: Van der Velde.* Of course we went, and were royally treated. I didn't entirely understand this special treatment until a few weeks ago, when all those Dutch-Canadian war-stories, Canadians as unforgotten

---

* Fat chance, I know, but if you read this, Klaus….

liberators, the flower-bedecked tanks rolling into Amsterdam, were screened by the CBC.

I met, on those Dutch boats taking us across the Atlantic and then, in September, back to Montreal again, three NYC law-students, Paul Meyer, Mel Bergheim, and somebody else, all three older and wiser than I. Why were they all so kind? So patient with that callow youth? You, Paul, especially.

Walked all day every day the first part of the summer in Paris, returning at night to a student demi-pension on the rue d'Assas. Spent all of Bastille Night trailing from one *rive gauche* (what other *rive* would it be?) café to another with a girl from Michigan whom I cared as little for as she for me, and decided the next morning that a change was in order. This turned out to be the first hitchhiking of my life. Back in university one of my profs had mentioned a book called *Mont St.Michel and Chartres*, strongly implying that every serious human being had read this book, or ought to, and as a step in the right direction I had bought it although I had not yet read it.* The title alone must, though, have influenced my choice of hitchhiking destinations. My journey began, on the advice of a student acquaintance, with a bus-ride to Versailles: better to start from there, this fellow had said (although he'd never tried to *faire l'auto-stop* himself), than from the chaos of a Parisian suburb. Just before noon, then , standing in the approved fashion with my hand, palm outwards, in the air at the southern end of Versailles, I was approached by a man who identified himself as a plainclothes policeman, and advised me that I was wasting my time. In postwar France, he said, nobody offers rides to anybody. It simply isn't done, he said: you never knew who you might be allowing into your car, into your life. I assured him that he was mistaken and that I'd soon be on my way, at which he nodded kindly but said he'd come back towards evening, would assuredly find me still in place and would convey me to his home where I could spend the night before returning the next morning, defeated, to Paris. He was just backing up his car to leave when a large *camion* pulled up, the door swung open and I was waved in.

What follows would be a triumphant *Hitchhiker's Guide to the*

Still haven't.

Ile de France and Bretagne, were it not for the fact that the *camion*-driver, a surly brute (he had a very young boy with him, a speechless child who dared not look at either of us and whom I have worried about a few hundred times since), said not a word for the next seventy miles before pulling up at a truckers café into which he signalled me to follow him. Did I have a choice? Apparently not. Once inside he informed me that I was to pay for his lunch, and, this seemed an afterthought, also for the lunches of the half-dozen other men, presumably all truckers, already sitting and eating there. I'm still not sure what would have happened next if it hadn't been that one of the seated men, without so much as moving in his chair, told this bully, not quietly, that he was *'un vrai bâtard'.* My few minutes in that café, I must tell you, are still with me in exact detail, so the following citations are dead on. The brute, obviously on the lowest rung of the café-hierarchy and unable or unwilling to cope with this unexpected character-analysis, muttered, *"Mais c'est moi qui l'emmène"*—"It's me who's taking him", which only brought forth another torrent of abuse from my life-and-honour-saving defender. *"T'es un 'tit morceau de merde, toi"* is the only line from his uninterrupted assault that, why not put it this way, sticks with me. And that was basically it. The rest of the onlookers, till then either on the fence or quite willing, it's my belief, to have this young interloper pay for their food, changed sides. The overmatched *bâtard* looked for a chair at the communal table, was waved off, slumped down at another table on his own, and the rest of them went back to their soups. Nobody spoke. I stood there haplessly for, I'll guess, a tenth of a minute—still nobody spoke to me nor I to anybody—and then turned and left. Outside felt quite a lot better. I was without lunch but that was just fine, my thin wallet was no thinner than before. Best of all, a few minutes later I was picked up by a likeable, courteous, prematurely balding, tweed-jacketed man driving a little Renault *deux-chevaux* who confessed (the confession probably only came after our talk had established my blatant harm-lessness) that during the war he had been a member of Pétain's *milice*, the Vichyite police. We talked nonstop en route to Chartres, not a word about the potentially controversial recent past but exclusively about (again I will claim that my recall is close to exact) classical French literature. I know that Bossuet's name came up, leaving no footprints,

but also the *penseurs* and moralists Amiel, Vauvenargues, and Cham-
fort, all of them intermittently mind-mining and securely establishing
(once I'd had a few years to build on what I heard during that drive
towards Chartres), as far as I'm concerned, that there's an impossibly
cool manner of wisdom-sharing that's distinctively French and
nobody else's. And Benjamin Constant, I first heard of him that day
too, and of his *Adolphe* which has since become my favourite novella
in all the world. And finally, a line I can't be altogether accurate in
quoting because I've never found it on a printed page, only heard it
in that little Renault on that long-ago day from the mouth of that
cultivated torturer, as perhaps he was: it's from Stendhal, who was
the *milicien*'s favourite author, and this is how it goes. "Rousseau was
unhappy all his life because he wanted to find the kind of friend of
which no more than ten, perhaps, have existed since the time of
Homer". I've thought of that a few times since. Quite a few times, to
speak plain. I know it to be a sad, wonderful line, a line which has
often, when without warning it floats near my mind, caused me to
pause in whatever I was doing and ponder it: ponder those ten, perhaps, friendships. What they would be like. Whether I had had any.
Whether I had ever been such a friend to anyone. When we'd reached
a place on that long and straight autostrade from which I could see
the towers of Chartres cathedral a mile or two, as I thought, ahead, I
asked to be let off, explaining to my third new friend of that day that
I hoped to have an unhurried, deliberate, drinking-it-all-in approach
to an iconic structure I might never have the chance to see again. Our
farewells were warm, he drove off, and I began what I thought would
be a half-hour trudge to the cathedral. It turned out, of course, that
those twin grey towers were easily fifteen miles off: it was like seeing
the Rockies from halfway across Alberta and deciding to cover the
distance on foot. No, not quite like that, but an *Ile de France* equivalent.
It was also where my Chartres miracle, or, better, my en-route-to-
Chartres miracle, took place. As I walked those five or six hours on
that warm and sun-filled day, between fields of golden corn peopled
with, believe this or not, peasants, or let me say persons in recognizable
peasant-gear, almost all of them girls and women and all of these
girls and women in long skirts and kerchiefs, scything the waving,
golden corn (maize?) as I walked past them, I had something as close

to an epiphany as my young life to that point had allowed me. Unbelievable, thinking back to that afternoon and that scene and my unlikely presence in it—it was like being in a Millet painting down to the last detail, it even showed not a few of those kerchiefed girls and women straightening up to wave at me as I passed. They were waving, I suppose, at the strangeness of this apparition, this unfamiliar lengthy boy carrying a duffel-bag and walking quite alone along that traffic-free road in the heat of that July day in 1948. The picture I was seeing on both sides as I walked is now so familiar to me, so composed—it hangs, as I have learned, on so many gallery walls, and is by either Millet (Jean-François,1814-1875), or, a painter I like much more than Millet, Camille Pissarro (1830-1903)—(Pissarro is probably my preferred French painter and must surely have more than once set up his easel or taken out his sketch-pad in just such golden fields as those I was walking past, and among just such gleaners and harvesters)—that it's hard to feel sure that all this could have happened, that this is really and truly how it looked and how it was. And that I was there, walking down the middle of it.

But it is and it was. And I was.

No, I did not roll up my sleeves and spend the rest of the afternoon scything away among them, nor did I, after a rustic feast and many a beaker full of the warm South, pass the night in some nearby barn in the brawny arms of Lisette or Marguerite.* Nevertheless my belief, that day, that I was only minutes away from the cathedral, and that it was therefore time to leave the *milicien*'s car and start walking, turned out to be one of the most blessed miscalculations of my life. The cathedral, its stained-glass windows at that time still blackened by their eight centuries of service, windows that sent smoky shadows up and down the dark and mysterious lengths of the north and south transepts (instead of as those windows are now, in 2007, bright and scrubbed and about as mysterious as a Holiday Inn) was worth every step of my long walk. But the walk is what I remember.

Of the rest of that journey, all I really have to report is this. At the last of my destinations, St.Michael's Mount, having run short of francs

---

*At that stage of my life I had not passed any nights in anybody's arms, brawny or otherwise.

and hence having spent the night bedless and wandering about, I was sitting on a rock at five in the morning looking out over the mile or two of tide-abandoned endless ribbed sand when a woman in a two-piece red bathing suit clambered past me down to the beach and then reappeared walking away from me westward toward the horizon, towards the miles of emptiness ahead. After the first hundred feet or so she took off her top and kept on going, holding the top in her hand and swinging it as she went, and I watched her until she'd become a distant point in the dawn.

She still does that now and then, that long saunter towards the far-off sea, the waiting tide.*

Back in Paris and having eaten my first meal in close to three days (I remember leaning, semi-conscious, against a bare brick wall en route to my pension, gathering strength for the final couple of *rues* to the rue d'Assas), I took note that it was the morning of the funeral of the novelist and Academician Georges Bernanos, of whom, naturally, I had never heard. I walked into the ceremony because dark purple flags bearing the inscription *Pompes Funèbres* in giant gold letters were fluttering triffid-like over the sidewalk, almost blocking my path. I stood respectfully in there enduring the acclaim and the lengthy explanations by Bernanos's pals of his behaviour during the Occupation—impeccable, it seemed to them to have been, even though he was writing and publishing with, mysteriously, no apparent hassle from either the S.S. or the Vichy police. Because our life-and-death had crossed in this way I bought, later that summer, a used copy of a novel of his called *Sous le Soleil de Satan*. It's still here. Also, that summer, met André Gide at a political rally for the *Mouvement Républicain Populaire*, being introduced to the Grand Old Man by the father of a student I'd met.

————

*Readers may think there's more dissimilarity than similarity between this Mont St.Michel anecdote and what I'm about to footnote it with, but here goes. In Thomas Mann's story *Death in Venice*, his protagonist, the famous composer Gustav von Aschenbach, is sitting in a deck-chair on the Lido beach watching a young boy playing at the water's edge. Aschenbach is old and right now, although he doesn't know it, he's dying, in fact he's only got two sentences of his life left, but as he watches the boy, whom he's in love with, "It seemed to him the pale and lovely Summoner out there smiled at him and beckoned…"

"M.Gide, un jeune Canadien."

"Enchanté".

Moi aussi, sort of.

Found, later that month, *Les Faux-Monnayeurs* and *Le Roi Candaule* in one of the boxes along the Seine. They're still here too, along with some later Gide acquisitions, his *Journals.*

Did not meet Alain-Fournier, the author of *Le Grand Meaulnes.* This was a thin novel I bought that summer and, because it fit my pocket, just kept on re-reading during my solitary lunches and metro-rides in those weeks. I didn't meet Alain-Fournier because he and a detachment of his men, during World War One, had walked into a woods one day and were never seen again.

Not unlike 'big Meaulnes', who vanishes in the woods of the world inside that novel and is vainly hunted for by the narrator.

And I discovered, very early in that summer, the *Jeu de Paume,* the Impressionist gallery (gone now, replaced by the far grander *Musée d'Orsay*) which may have given me the most meaningful visual-art walk-through of my life, room after chronologically-ranked room past all those barely-heard-of names. Before I left Paris I spent a few hours at *Braun et cie,* among whose prints and reproductions of everything the *Jeu de Paume* possessed you could browse as freely and as long as you wished, and where I bought, for the equivalent of a few dollars, a Gauguin I've never liked, a Matisse of two bare-armed girls in what the English call frocks, and a storm scene of Vlaminck's, my favourite of the three and the only one that's gone missing over the intervening 50-plus years.

It was 1948, which was *the* existentialist summer, but I never saw any of the stars, never shook a Gauloise out of the pack onto a *terrasse* table near Sartre or de Beauvoir or Greco. They knew we were there and kept changing their bistros—the *Flore,* the *Deux Magots,* the *Tabou,* it was hard to keep up. Speaking of seeing the *illustrés* of that time and place, I did, though, get to see and hear, live, some of the club singers I would keep on listening to for years and years after that

---

[cont'd...]

Nothing similar at all, really. Some kind of raggedy-edged asymmetry has obviously got into my head.

summer's end, until long after they'd outgrown the little *boîtes* and cabarets they could be seen and heard in during those nights. This probably started with Montand (*Les Feuilles Mortes*, what else) and graduated through Dany Dauberson and Jean-Claude D'Arnal and a few more, to the one I still listen to as in the very temple, yes, of Delight. This was and is Georges Brassens, and the songs would be *Dans l'eau de la claire fontaine* and *Au bois de mon coeur* and, even more than those darkling two, *L'Auvergnat*, which is a song he sings to an unknown woman who gave him bread and shelter when all the '*gens bien-intentionés*' shut their doors on him.

Deep sad guitar, ditto voice. 'Plangent', both of them, really, but that was one of my twice-a-week teen-age words, it's had a Hold on it for too long to be re-activated now.

I didn't see Camus, either, not then, but I did buy *L'Étranger*, a book which will always be for me *the* emblematic novel of my youth, and the only one whose first page I can still recite from memory. And Camus himself…ah, I have many another tale of him, did I but want to tell them.

I do want. (Even though I know, I know, tales of him exist here already. Surely this one's the last.)

Ten years after that first summer in France, on a brief tour of Normandy, walking into the first French war cemetery I'd ever entered, the name on the first cross I saw was CAMUS. This is true. *The very first one. Just inside the gate.*

I knew, by that time, that Albert's father had been killed in WWI, but I also knew, and was sorry that I knew (I forget how I knew; there were no initials on that cross, and no first name, so that wasn't the reason I knew; but I did know) that this couldn't be him. Couldn't be he.

Albert's favourite words: mother, honour, *misère*, summer, sea.*

His best book: *La Chute*. A man in a bar in a foreign city, Amsterdam, actually, tells a stranger of the time he was walking across a bridge over the Seine in a fog and saw a girl standing by the railing. He goes on to tell him how he wondered why she was there, alone in

---

*Here's an inexact but interesting comparison with Flaubert, who wrote: "The finest three things in creation are the sea, Hamlet, and Mozart's Don Giovanni."

the fog, and how, a few minutes later, he heard a splash. He paused then, he tells the stranger, but continued walking. He thinks about this often, he says.

And Ian McEwan wins the Booker a few years ago with a novel called *Amsterdam* which makes much use of a man who cannot forget that he watched, from a safely hidden place, a scene which led on to a girl's death, when a little bravery, an intervention, might have saved her. No reviewer of *Amsterdam* mentions *La Chute*.

No blame (of McEwan) is intended here. Just that it would be nice to live in a time and place where such things, in this case the Camus/McEwan Amsterdam/*mauvaise-foi* connection, get noticed, where you could count on at least one reviewer noticing it.

A last couple of lines from Camus's *Notebooks*. Or…um, not. I have quoted these lines a bunch of times, to others or to myself, but now I cannot find them. Very mysterious: I've leafed every page of the *Notebooks*. Have I imagined them? Are they my lines and not Camus's? No way. Not a syllable of them sounds like me. Which doesn't mean I disagree with either of them.

But the unfindable lines, wherever they are, read very much, I know this, as follows: "I would give up, anytime, the chance to have dinner with Albert Einstein for an initial rendezvous with a pretty chorus-girl". And, "The young girls laugh and chatter on the seashore, but he who watches them loses the right to speak to them."

And the right to speak *of* them, I sometimes think. When I do, it can seem a failure in…something. Tact? Yes, well, if it is then there are a few such failures here, for which here's my only defence: everything you read here, except for events of the very early years, happened to me or came into my mind during my third decade, *aetatis* 20-29. And through all of those years the world kept on seeming, day after day, new and inviting, and every street, even the rainy ones, seemed to have saved up a special glance.

That's just how it was, the only other direction I might go in describing it would be book-length and boring.

3.

Is ANYTHING beginning to happen here? Anything that might relate to an individual's initially-unacknowledged, then sensed, glimpsed, tested here and there, even seen wholly in flashes—something suggesting a gradual 'education', sentimental or otherwise?

4.

FINAL CURTAIN-CALL by Camus: *The people one day applauded him, which caused Phocion to remark: "Have I said something stupid?"*

5.

So I HADN'T GOT TO OXFORD in the way I'd wanted; I went to Cambridge instead. Though not before I'd spent a year in London working in a bookshop on Borough High Street in Southwark, just steps from the Thames, and steps from the Pool of London, where salt-encrusted vessels with Conradian names and flying Panamanian and Liberian flags docked, stayed for a week or so, and vanished as pointlessly, or so it seemed, as they'd arrived. Half of our bookshop-clientele were seamen from that 'Pool', visiting us in search of English-Hindustani dictionaries. The other half were students from Guy's Hospital, which was only streets away, and for whom we stocked the medical texts they needed. I remember the manager and I, one morning, trundling a barrowload of such texts to Guy's where we set up shop in a ground-floor corridor. So, medical texts and conversation-aids, and thin packets of even thinner carbon paper, and that was about it, that was our stock. Hatchard's we were not, Foyle's we were also not; Waterstone's, well, they were decades off still.

What we did have, however, in addition to the texts, etc, (though no one but the manager and I, his sole employee, knew of this) were simply those books which the two of us wanted for our own purposes, wanted, right away, as soon as possible, to read. This would come about thusly. When the 'travelers', i.e. the publishers' salesmen, arrived to take our orders, those Hindustani-English texts, those medical handbooks, that manager and I (foolish to keep on calling him 'the manager', as if this is a Kafka tale: his name was John Rolph, he was only a few years older than I, and he was a poet who owned a small press, called The Scorpion Press, which produced chapbooks of poetry, some of these by people later to become quite well known, Bernard Kops for one, Jon Silkin, maybe, for another) would order from these travelers any book or books we happened in that week to wish to read. Payment for these went on the shop's account, need it be said. A week or so later the books, neatly parcelled, would be delivered by H.M. Mail. We would open these parcels, divide the spoils, and over the next week or two, during the long undisturbed mornings and most of the rest of the day as well, we would sit in a very small room at the back of the shop, each tilted back in his mutilated, two-or-three-legged Dickensian armchair, feet on a chipped wooden table, on winter days with an electric heater on that table between us, and....*read*. Yes, Reader, that's what we did. We read, I suppose, for seven or eight hours each day; pulling the metallic screen down over the shopfront (the shop had no door: the front of it was open to the weather between 8 a.m. and 6 p.m.) at day's-end, hoisting it again the following morning at eight; and in between hoisting and lowering, *reading*. That winter, I don't remember why this was so but it was, I bought (well, ordered) and read nothing but works on mysticism. Swedenborg, St. John of the Cross, *The Interior Castle* of St. Teresa of Avila, William Law's *A Serious Call to a Devout and Holy Life* (that brave title!), Jakob Boehme's *The Signature of All Things*, the 'Theologica Germanica', Boethius's *Consolation*...that's not the end of it. The mysticism press's salesman must have thought he'd died and joined the ineffable ones. Sixteen years later in Toronto I would be 'teaching', as we say, *The Interior Castle* at York University: Teresa wasn't my favourite, that was the shoemaker Jakob Boehme, but I remember thinking that the latter wouldn't be happy on a university course, too gentle and too sweet, I thought, best to spare him that. "And he will come to meet thee in thy mind"—I always liked his insistence on these *mind*-meetings, I always felt it was no accident that that phrase kept surfacing. It suggested a quiet distancing on the shoemaker's part from the literal/corporeal stuff that so many churchgoers both

179

then and later favoured, the flaunted Galilean *rencontres*.

Teresa, though, was durable, I guessed she'd survive any seminar. Good guess.

John, during those long wintry afternoons, would usually be reading from the stack of hopeful and unsolicited MSS the mail kept on bringing addressed to *The Scorpion Press*. "What d'you think of this, then?" he'd ask, and I'd lower my shoemaker for a bit and listen. I'd had little interest in poetry up until those *ad hoc* seminars. By the time that year was ending, though, having passed through various stages from humble-listener to increasingly assured, increasingly nonchalant judge of lots of pages of verse, that had changed.

How did we get away with these semi-solitary readings, these surreal book-order-sheets?* We got away with it because the shop was one of a chain, the chain was drifting, perhaps already foundering, and nobody from head office, if there was such a thing, ever arrived to check on us. Loyalty we did *not* feel, granted these impersonal circumstances, and granted, too, our minuscule wages. As far as both of us were concerned, we were ships that pass. John was readying himself for better things (his 'better thing' was, a year or so later, an antique-booksellers' business of his own, which he still maintains in a former coach-house on the main street of a seaside town in Suffolk. He stocks no medical texts and no English-Hindustani dictionaries). I was a rowboat passing the Pool of London, the endless wharfs and docklands of the great city, in a drowsy afternoon.

I remember the two of us having lunch one day in a steamy fish-and-chips shop, when John told me he had been offered sole European commercial rights to the famous photo of the smiling kneeling naked Marilyn Monroe. Showing me the photo, which was not yet famous, he asked me if he should accept this offer, what did I think of the ethical issue involved. I was fairly well stunned by the question but upon being pressed I said, well, maybe you shouldn't. I admired him, I thought he shouldn't. *Noblesse oblige* is maybe what I thought. Whether it was because I said this or on the basis of some further reasoning of his own, he didn't.

Could it have made his fortune, if he had? No, but it could have

---

*granted the nature of our clientele, they *were* surreal.   .

earned him a couple of years gazing over his typewriter at the Bay of Biscay, maybe. Was my advice priggish? Maybe. Was it a totally alien decade, the Fifties, alien to this present decade in terms of both the question and the response? Bet your life.

Clincher: I often lunched, that year, with another young writer, a Scot called, of all things, Jock, in a kind of student café such as Paris has always had many more of than London, but this was nevertheless in London and the students mostly from Guy's Hospital. One of the reasons we met in this particular café was that Jock greatly admired a very goodlooking blonde called Georgina who waitressed there. Georgina had lovely eyes and breasts and always kept a special one (eye) on us, refilling our plates when she ought not to have, and I was just as impressed as Jock was by the several things concerning her which I have mentioned, but Jock had seen her first, *basta così.** From him came a question not unlike the Marilyn Monroe query. Jock was writing a multi-stanza'd love poem, and although he would, of course, never identify the beloved inside any of those stanzas, in fact he was always thinking of Georgina, he told me, while he wrote. His problem was that he was married and had no intention of leaving his wife or of ever suggesting any sort of clandestine activity to or with Georgina. He would never do this even though he was pretty sure, he told me, that he was in love with Georgina. Jock's question was, what did I think of the morality of *thinking about* Georgina while he worked on his poem.

This nonplussed me even more than the Marilyn Monroe conundrum. These people were made of much finer stuff than I was, was what I remember deciding. In this case I said that I thought it was OK. Think away, Jock.

Generous of me.

An alien decade for sure.

_____

*'nuff said

6.

JUST ONE MORE anecdote from my indentured eight months in the bookselling trade. It's an important one in this early-life story, although it's only brought to mind by the double-page spread on visual art in last Saturday's *Guardian* (issue of 16.12.06). The spread featured the work of Euan Uglow, a painter of whom I had not heard but whose unsentimental, stripped-away (flaking, like an old fresco, is the impression they give) images are going to stay with me for a long while. His surname is why this story's here. John Rolph had a friend of that name, John Uglow (when I first heard it I thought the name an unlucky one, the glow at its end not quite managing to brighten the opening ugliness), who ran a secondhand bookshop not far from our own humble quarters—and one day John had a phone call asking him to come to the Uglow shop sharpish. When he asked if he might bring a friend, this was agreed to, and about a minute past six, as soon as we had brought our pseudo-door clattering down, we set off. It turned out that John Uglow was leaving the business, that he had sold the contents of his shop to "thieves" (he felt he'd been grossly underpaid in the transaction and suspected that the buyers would be selling the stock off on a by-weight basis; hence his eagerness to show his books such honour as he could by involving his friend John Rolph and, as it happened, me, in his shop's final hours). We arrived at the cellar-level shop, opened the first of two bottles we had bought en route, and spent the next several hours talking, drinking , and going through those library-like stacks which must have held thousands upon thousands of books, hardly one of which deserved their arranged fate. A fate they would not escape unless, as John U. kept on reminding us, we added more of them, and then still more, and more again, to the various baskets and bags he had ready for our use. Of payment he would accept none: we were doing him a favour, he insisted, in preserving for as many as possible of his books an ongoing and respected life. As for us, we tried to at least stem this generosity, we were ready to leave after we'd picked out our first seven or eight titles and stacked them beside a free piece of wall. To no avail. I could go downstairs in my North Toronto house right now and identify, among my books, oh, seventy-five from that Uglowtrove: Jeremy Taylor's leatherbound works, a broken set but with the critical bits intact; three volumes from 'Bohn's Antiquarian Library' (5/- per volume) of the wonderful Sir Thomas Browne ("Man is a noble animal, splendid in ashes and pompous in the grave...", or, no less beloved of the hobbling and veering fraternity I've lately signed on with, "What song the Syrens sang, or what name Achilles assumed when he hid himself among women, though puzzling questions, are not beyond all conjecture"); a clutch of Waugh novels; the faded-pink *complete* works of Thos. Carlyle (the handsome bookplates inside the front covers show they were once the property of "Hugh Steven", who bought the books from "David Bryce and Son, Glasgow" in 1897, the year of my parents' births); an early and very thin cardboard-bound volume of Yeats...the foundations of a modest library, in fact, and certainly the true origin of my own present several walls of books. "No, no, you haven't even *looked* down this aisle yet!" John U. would cry, as we attempted to sidle away (sidling was not easy with those mounting stacks of books, those bulging bags).

So it was. We all eventually went off and feasted, not expensively or well, but lengthily, at a pub around the corner from Southwark Cathedral, and then all went back and climbed, *mit Bücher*, into a cab and careened off to our various addresses. I feel an undiminished affection for John Uglow, a small squat man with bulgey eyes and an indignant heart, whom I thought of this week because of Euan, probably no relative although I hope he may be such, since I like his paintings well enough to associate him with the little bookseller who carried on his business just off the High Street in the Royal Borough of Southwark and, to identify the region of his working life more familiarly although less grandly, the Pool of London.

7. Ronnie Scott's Club and Mary

HE FIRST MET MARY at very close quarters in the cupboard-sized 'studio' in which Len Williams, the father of the later-world-famous guitarist John Williams (Segovia's favourite pupil), gave them the first of a set of six one-hour lessons on the guitar. £1 per lesson, a snip at £5 the set. He and Mary were the only ones to have registered for the course. On guitars loaned gratis by Len they began learning to pluck forth nursery-level versions of Romanze, the beautiful Spanish lyric which pours off the screen so movingly as the camera-eye rises to the iron rafters of the Gare du Nord in the closing scene of the equally-beautiful postwar French film called *Les Jeux Interdits*, translated as 'The Secret Game'. Mary's knee pressed his, or his hers, for the whole of that first lesson, neither of those knees budging from a contact they could not have avoided if they'd tried and neither of them tried. Neither Mary nor he even spoke to each other the whole time, just the knees, the growing cordiality of the two knees as the hour went on, and when they left the tiny room, which was at the top of a steep staircase exiting into Frith Street, he carried her piggyback, death for two if he'd stumbled, down the vertiginous unbannistered staircase into the street, and thence into a coffeeshop, awful in its charmlessness, the clouds of steam from the counter, the waiter's distracted swipe at their table with a suspect washcloth. And two weeks later, as Robert Musil cleverly writes in *The Man Without Qualities*, which might be the 4th or 5th-best novel in the world, they had been lovers for a fortnight.

From the second week onwards, as soon as class was out they'd head straight across Frith Street and into Ronnie Scott's, the famous jazz club where Johnny Dankworth led the house band, and where Cleo Laine was just beginning to make her reputation singing with that band, and later on as everybody knows marrying JD. Cleo and JD are still together, it's good to report, which is more than can be said about Mary and him.

Which is too bad, in a way. Because although Mary was divorced and unhappy, nothing new there, and childless, and not beautiful either although those legs of which the knees were such an unmissable part would have graced the Crazy Horse Saloon or the *Folies Bergères* in Paris or, if you wanted to go down-market and keep the legs in London, the Windmill, she was serious and thoughtful and so un-selfish, he used to say, that he could hardly bear, he used to say, to remember how little he gave her in return. But he did manage to bear it, didn't he.

8.

CONTRASTING THAT 1950's London with present-day Europe, present-day U.K. and particularly present-day London (awash in tourists, traffic, tiny-talent Turner Prizes, and 30-year-old multimillionaires moving rupees and yen and dollars and deutschmarks into and out of little boxes on their computer screens in one financial institution or another, and a musical called *Jerry Springer*), I'm grateful to have been there when I was. I'm aware that the decade's passed into history, into myth, as dull and drab, a kind of *salle d'attente* for the glittering Sixties, everybody putting significant life on hold until Mary Quant and the Beatles would show up to break the spell; and it's certainly true that London wasn't cool then, it was still dealing with vistas of wildflowers growing out of bombed acres of tumbled bricks and entire blocks of loose stone and plaster and masonry. For me, though, it's "the innocence and modesty of those years"* that I choose to remem-ber when I think my way back to them. I'm talking about and from the privileged, or cloistered, or clouded state of being young, obviously, but there was, I'm pretty sure, a more general sense of a waiting-to-happen that was in the *Zeitgeist*, the spirit of the time—it wasn't just the young, I think, who noticed that almost anything that occurred to you as worth doing, worth trying, worth travelling to, had a realistic content in those years: that is, you could *afford* to do it or try it or travel to it. You could touch the city at its heart (I mean, by that swampy phrase, that you could see any play at the cost of a shilling or two for a seat in any theatre's upper circle; the art galleries were free; the opera at Covent Garden was...not free but at least there were standing-room places and No, they were *not* all corporate-booked

Having It So Good: Britain in the Fifties, by Peter Hennesey (Allen Lane, 2007)

years ahead—that particular obscenity was unknown). For threepence you could travel the shortest underground routes and for sixpences or shillings instead of multi-pounds you could go long distances overground. You could manage all these for some small portion of your apparently, in today's terms, pitiable pay-packet. I was paid £5 5s. a week by my bookshop-employers, Grattan's—I really doubt if there were too many people in the labour force who were earning less than that—but my four-staircases-up flat in Notting Hill cost me only a fifth of that, a guinea a week.

Another retrieval from that London year. I'd discovered, at the top of Charing Cross Road, an art-bookshop-cum-gallery called Zwemmer's, and I often spent an hour or two there on a Saturday. Zwemmer's may have been the leading purveyor of expensive art-books in the world in 1954. It has a walk-on role in one of the most character-istic passages in Cyril Connolly's *The Unquiet Grave*, a thin book of *pensées*, epigrams, laments that had a big effect on me in those years, much bigger, I'll suppose, that I'd allow it to have today if I were to come freshly to it. Good that I'm not coming freshly to it today! I'd have missed out on so many early states of mind and odd juvenile meditations that I can now so easily call back from that half-century-ago self. Here's the Connolly passage.

August 7th: the first full autumn day. Walked to the bookshop at closing time. Raining. A girl tried to get into the shop, but the doors were bolted. Went out and followed her past the Zwemmer Gallery and through the streets towards St.Giles', only to lose her by the Cambridge Theatre…Much disturbed by the incident, for this girl, with her highforehead, her pointed nose, her full lips and fine eyes, her dark hair and her unhappy and sullen expression, personified both beauty and intelligence. She was bare-legged,and wore sandals, a green corduroy suit and a linen coat…. "O toi qui j'eusse aimée."

Funny, memories like that. There's a not-dissimilar one elsewhere in this book, one that I have the Connolly rôle in. Odd, how they linger through the years, how lucidly this one burns. Philip Larkin, who after Edward Thomas is in my view the finest English-language poet of the 20th century*—well, no, he's a greater poet than Thomas,

---

*No, I haven't forgotten Yeats, I just decided not to complicate the page by mentioning him.

only he doesn't quite make it into me to the same quietly private depth—at a first meeting with Cyril Connolly, said, referring to *The Unquiet Grave,* "Sir, you formed me".

I don't know what Connolly had to say to that, he was given to vicious *ripostes* so maybe it's just as well his biographer doesn't tell us; but I understand Larkin's saying what he did. Posturing and sentimental and florid as Connolly often is, it's precisely his willingness to be such things, to put them in print, that draws one to him, that gives such scenes as this one, the dark girl with her sullen expression on a rainy late-afternoon by the Cambridge Theatre, such enduring life. A scene that is lost forever! and the actors in that scene so unmourned! How, you feel (or *I* feel), can a so-intensely rendered minute be so tracelessly gone?

Well, it's *not* gone, of course, is it.

Many of that decade's better-known one-liners are Connolly's. From his *Enemies of Promise,* a book which famously names, among the probable 'enemies' of a young writer's promise, "the baby-carriage in the front hall", comes also the dictum, aimed primarily as himself (since he had, he felt, taken on too many book-reviews, written too many book-page editorials, undertaken too much journalism generally), "Anyone who's at work on anything less than his masterpiece is his own fool". And, most quoted of all, also aimed at himself, "Inside every fat man a thin one is wildly signalling to be let out". 142 pages are all there are in *The Unquiet Grave*—about twenty pages more than perfection, probably, but I wouldn't want to lose more than that from this uniquely honed exercise in nostalgia.

But it is for, finally, his full-hearted offering of love for the works of others that Connolly has his place in my pantheon. *"I have loved poetry all my life. I remain the ideal lecteur for the poets whom I understand, for I am a sound box, a record player, an Aeolian harp who gathers up and stores innumerable fragments, and for me to love the poem is to love the poet who wrote it and become his man."*

Any writer, even one with only the most modest expectations of the way the world will attend to him, to her, must be moved by this claim, this confession. To have a hundred who feel so about one's work— — to have, but have in all truth, ten— —

9.

LAST LONDON GLIMPSE. In that Olden Tyme you could, and I did, walk into the St.Martin's School of Art at the foot of Charing Cross Road, minutes from Leicester Square and Trafalgar Square and Covent Garden, and once inside (no one asked what you were about as you went in) you could wander the warren of rooms and studios, observe here and there a *Maître*-to-be (the young Lucian Freud, maybe—I've no idea if he ever was near the place, but he could have been, the dates are right), check the bulletin boards for upcoming shows of students' work, for rentable ateliers or Soho flats, single or shared, same-or-varied-sex, or even, no qualifications required, you could sign up for a course in painting or drawing or sculpting. Such a course cost so little I'm best off not telling, you'd be doubting everything else I have to say. For a while, in the undarkening spring of that distance-dazzled year of my life, when things were slow at the South-wark shop and John was content to have his cubbyhole reading-room to himself, I attended, several mornings a week, a life-drawing class at St.Martin's. The class numbered 17 or 18 persons, most of them girls (it's what they called themselves: Germaine Greer wasn't around yet to alert them to the offensiveness of the description) and most of them as openminded and openhearted concerning whoever might be standing beside them in that untidy studio as anyone could wish or ask. Each of us stood at one of that room's several levels with her or his easel and floppy pad of large-format paper and soft black pencil, and for the better part of two-and-a-half hours did rapid-fire sketches of the model of the day, whoever that might be. Ours alternated between a geriatric gent who would usually arrive late and shaky with his clattering empty wine bottles in a brown paper carrier-bag, bring-ing with him a face the many crevasses and chasms of which only the blackest tool in your kit could hint at—he looked like a Dürer knight on his way home from a last crusade (or like, to disinflate that sorry image, an old man with too many rainy nights on a park bench behind him)—between him, as I was saying, and Beatrice Kajan, a truly lovely woman with legs she liked to mock as 'columns' but a Madonna face (the Fra Angelico sort, not the tabloid gargoyle who may already be announcing herself to your imagination) and black braids who several times had some of us to parties in the Hampstead flat her elderly admirer kept her in, or thought he did. Bea, we all liked you lots.

Our drawing-master, whose name I can't recover, once had me to dinner at his home with his wife and himself, and then took me to a meeting and lecture at the Royal Academy, of which he was, if it need be said, a member. A kind man, a kind act. I didn't know why I was at the R.A.'s Burlington House home that evening but I did know that I was paying close attention to everything that moved or didn't move in that elegant room—to the sonorities from the podium, to the portraits of bygone Presidents (i.e. the Reynoldses and the Gainsboroughs and—not sure about this one—the Constables), and to the certainty that I was in a privileged enclave of this multi-centuried culture and I'd never be in it again.

I was right about that. Still remember it though, as you see.

In that St.Martin's class: a perfect, as they say, English rose, member of the Kentish squirearchy; in today's terminology she'd be a Sloanie. We went to the first English-language production of *Waiting for Godot*, which I think was at the Criterion Theatre in Piccadilly Circus. I knew the actor playing Estragon, hence our classy tickets in the orchestra. It may have been the girl from Kent's first time in a theatre: she wore a large-brimmed and beribboned hat, it would have been perfect for a garden-party and she looked even more English-rose than usual wearing it, but I don't know what the people trying to see the stage from the row behind her thought of it.

No complaints from them though. They may have been as dumbstruck as most of the London critics were by Estragon, Vladimir, Pozzo, Lucky, and Godot's little boy.

"Let's go!"

They do not move.

10.

I, HOWEVER, moved. To Stockholm.

11. Bodil

He had just got off the boat in Gothenburg, having arrived in this unpremeditated country because a Toronto acquaintance had shown up in London driving a big red Thunderbird which came complete with an expensive German girlfriend, and had said "Come to Stockholm". There was no reason why not. That first evening in Stockholm, his acquaintance plus expensive girlfriend doing whatever they were doing, he wondering where he'd sleep the next night (he certainly couldn't afford to stay where all three of them had temporarily put up), he'd gone for a long wander, ending up in the Old Town, called *Gamla Stan*. It was about 7.30 in a soft October evening and he found himself in a narrow cobbled street, a street he seemed to have all on his own, until he began hearing the clack of a woman's heels from the far end of it. Eventually he saw her emerging from the shadows, and then she was close, longlegged and of course, pretty, and she said something to him. Later on he'd know what it was she said, she was asking a question as to where a certain *gata*, street, was—at the time, though, all he could do was say he didn't speak Swedish. She said that was all right because she spoke a little English. In English, then, she asked her question, and he explained that as this was his absolutely first night in her country, he couldn't even name the street they were in. She smiled and hesitated and then looked ready to continue her walk, perhaps she hadn't been so unsure of how to get to that *gata* after all, but at this point he felt he'd already stretched his capacity for stupidity* beyond anything bearable so he said he now had a question for her, if she didn't mind. She didn't mind. After tonight, he told her, he would be homeless, and he thought that he might be looking for a flat, somewhere he could stay for a few weeks, maybe even longer, he said—and he asked if she had any thoughts about this, how he might set about his looking. She said that if he'd continue straight on a bit he would very soon find himself kitty-corner from a *konditori*, café, which was owned by her mother, and if he would go

---

*This might be my only chance to quote a line I like from Paul Valéry, in whose short story, 'La Soirée avec M.Teste,' we meet the eponymous Teste, whose opening line is "La bêtise n'est pas mon fort".

in there and wait just a little she'd be back from her errand and see if she could help. This was agreed and she walked on, and so did he.

He found the *konditori*, which was large, lots of mostly-empty tables, and he sat down and ordered a coffee. Before long the girl returned, took a newspaper from a rack on a counter, and sat down with him. He noticed a woman moving about and chatting here and there with the clientele but also keeping an eye on the two of them, but that was all he noticed along that line. They looked through the pages listing flats and rooms and didn't find anything long-term— by this time he'd told her he might stay until Christmas. They did, however, find a flat that was available for a fortnight and the girl called the number and set up an appointment for him for the next morning. As it turned out the flat was OK and he took it. Walking around the following couple of days the town seemed to him beautiful and full of English-speakers (he later learned that the Swedish highschools had taught German as the basic second language until 1944, at which time they had prudently switched to English, so you could usually tell a person's approximate age by the language he or she knew in addition to his or her native Swedish. For instance, this being 1955, if the person you'd met was twenty or so, her or his English was probably good; if older than that, best to try German with them or find someone else to talk to). On the third day of his life in Sweden the girl from the Gamla Stan *konditori* phoned him and they went out to what was called a dance club. The table they were given was large and round and exclusively, except for him, occupied by women, all in their thirties or forties except for his date, who was much younger, perhaps 19, and much better-looking, and whose name, he by now knew, was Bodil, pron. *Bo*-deel. The other women at the table were obviously not at all pleased that Bodil had brought a date to the table, which made them seem wallflowers instead of simply women who sat at a table reserved for women. Also they may have been upset that she was so young and so pretty, what with her curly lightbrown hair and big soft eyes. The good thing was, though, that these other women spoke little or no English, as see above, so Bodil and he could speak as freely as they chose, or as freely as Bodil could go along with, i.e. not badly. They got on well, she was a fine dancer, which he was not, but his timing wasn't bad and she seemed happy to be able to show him one or two steps he didn't know. There were plenty of those, he told her. Near the end of their stay in that club, which was called the Bal Palais, Bodil told him that her parents had a small one-room house which was situated in the courtyard of the much larger house which the family lived in. The one-room house had once been used by her much older brother, who had wanted to be independent, she said, but now it had been unoccupied for years. It had no heating but there was a little old woman servant who, if he were to try living in that house, would come in early every morning in the winter and light a fire in his fireplace. He had told her he hoped to become a writer and she said that the little house would suit him very well. It might suit him *ütmärkt*, she said, meaning excellent or excellently. There was a table, a chair, a bed, a washroom with shower and toilet, and he'd be undisturbed in there, and, of course, warm. It would cost him nothing. The next day he went, by arrangement, to see the house in Bodil's parents' courtyard. Bodil's parents were both there, they seemed a little uncertain about this but had obviously made up their minds, probably after quite a lot of family discussion, that if he didn't turn them entirely off at first sight, if there wasn't any self-eliminating awfulness about him, they would go along with this for a while. Bodil's father was the mayor of the suburb in which their house was situated. This account won't mention the name of the suburb. He told the mayor and his wife that he was very appreciative of all this and that when his current arrangements ended in a week's time he would try it, but only on the understanding that if they wanted him out right away or soon, or if he wanted out, there would be no problem either way.

He did move into the little house, moving being a very simple matter since all he owned was in one soft fold-up bag plus his Olivetti portable, but he only stayed there a few days before deciding that there was something about it he didn't feel comfortable with. The little house looked and probably was very freshly scrubbed and the furnishings were fine, table, chair, bed, it was all *ütmärkt*, but it reminded him of a children's nursery rhyme or a Grimm Brothers tale maybe, which was of course absurd but there it was, it had reminded him of this and so it was how he felt. Bodil's parents were, he thought, not unhappy about his decision not to stay, although

Bodil was disappointed. The two of them went out on dates together for a couple of weeks after that and then he told her he'd found a place high up on Norr Mälarstrand, overlooking the Mälar-Sea and the West Bridge, a one-room apartment which a woman who wintered in Italy owned, and who wanted not very much rent in exchange for a reliable tenant. Which the mayor, Bodil's father, testified that he was. He told Bodil that he was going to need a lot of time to get his book on track, and that he'd found some translating work, a Spaniard he'd met called Luis had a sort of agency and he was doing French-into-English business letters for Luis, time-consuming but OK (later on, thanks to a Berlitz course he had signed up for, he would manage Swedish into English also) but what this all meant, he said, was that he wouldn't be able to call for a while. He never saw Bodil again and he was relieved that this was so, because he liked her and running into her later on would have been awkward. She was very nice, he thought, and of course very pretty, but perhaps a little young, although she had said this was not so, people her own age were so dull, and besides he was not so old, etc. And it's true, he wasn't. Still, he was sorry about it, in some unexamined way, and he never forgot her.

He never got to see the little old woman who would have made and lit fires for him. The days were still warm when he'd been in the small house in the courtyard, so there'd never been the need.

12.

UNINTEGRATED wrap-ups of the Swedish portion of this memoir:

The paintings of Edvard Munch, of which, although Munch was Norwegian, Swedish galleries have roomsful. Mostly picturing people on their own or being ignored by anyone else inside the frame. Munch, I think, chose loneliness above anything more complicated, and people who love his work do so because they know they can count on it to be like that, they can rely on it not to turn their minds back towards the uncertainties that the addition of another person to the same picture might remind them of. Hence all the paintings of a person alone, so often a woman looking out over water, with the moon shining a silver path on the water, her face turned away from us. It's important that her face is turned away like that, it underlines her preference not to be known, not even (which we would do, if her face were visible) to be guessed at.

The two Hjalmars, Gullberg and Söderberg: Gullberg's long poem called Gold-rain, and Söderberg's *Doktor Glas*, which I was given as an aid to learning Swedish during my first months there. In Swedish, which is the only way to really experience it (sorry, but it's so), it's almost as bare and pure as, say, Flaubert's *Un Coeur Simple*. And you can't get any purer than that.

I have also to mention, even though I did *not* discover him during the youthful decade this project is attempting to restrict itself to, Tomas Tranströmer, who is the finest Swedish poet I have ever read. He should be a Nobelist any year now, and even as I write this I think (since Tomas, who with his wife Monica is now a friend of mine, is about my age and is not well)... *why do we delay?**

Jüssi Björling's silken-voiced tenor singing *Ack Värmland Du Sköna* (Oh Warmland you beautiful) or *När Jag för Mig Själv in Mörka Skogen Går* (When I All Alone Go Through the Dark Woods).

Jarl Kulle, my favourite male Swedish actor, occasional *chansonnier*, the *beau idéal* of many a young Swede.

The sculptures along the water as you walk from the National Gallery towards the Thielska Gallery or Skansen or the Prinz Eugen gallery in Waldemarsudde, and the triumphant blue-and-yellow of the Swedish flag rippling against the bright blue sky in summer or late Spring, after its tactless, mocking appearance throughout the interminable grey winter. Which brings to mind also: the thousands of office workers standing in the first rays of the April sun with their backs against the grey stone buildings at noon in downtown Stockholm, faces tilted up, all that hunger.

Elizabeth Schwarzkopf, singing in the Konserthus, beautiful voice, beautiful woman. I fell for her as tens of thousands, no doubt, had done before me, some of them, I'll assume, with more realistic expectations than mine. Not many years before, she had sung for Hitler, for Goebbels. Dietrich Fischer-Dieskau coming into town not

---

*The God-voices, in *Oedipus at Colonus*

long after her, on his post-war way up, with Gerald Moore, the finest accompanist I ever heard. And beyond either of these, not in genius, probably, but in my pliant heart, Amalia Rodrigues singing *fados* in the Berns nightclub. A friend and I sat every night of her stint there, a week maybe, sat at the corner table of a balcony which actually overhung the stage, applauding as if we were showering the stage with flowers, with lovenotes, permitted to be there for the price of a few bottles of Tüborg, until she began noticing us and would tilt her face up and send us smiles we imagined to be as emotion-laden as our bravos truly were. Embarrassing to remember, but...not very.

And then there's the 90-year-old Bo Bergman, poet, longtime friend of Hjalmar Söderberg, and sometime drama critic for *Dagens Nyheter,* the leading Stockholm newspaper. Bo had known and "quite liked" Strindberg although he disliked almost all of his plays—except for *The Father,* which he "also disliked" but said he "knew", watching its first-night, "was a masterpiece". Bo lived on the same staircase that I, for a few months, was apartment-sitting in, and took to inviting me in to see his collection of ancient charts and maps—rolled-up papyrus-like guesses at the skies above and the seas surrounding the far more expansive Sverige of olden time, the immaculately-penned guesses of that time's illustrious astronomers and mariners. The visits entranced me, nothing less than that, the cracklings of the maps and charts as Bo unrolled them on the highly polished wood of his dining table are as fresh to my mind as the random sounds I hear now as I sit at my computer. We always finished a half-bottle of very old port during my visits in that apartment and I would stay not more than an hour because Bo tired easily and in spite of his very great courtesy, and the energies these showings clearly brought from him, he couldn't hide the fact. He was and will always be for me *sui generis,* and I'm grateful to fate for permitting us to meet, the odds against being what they were. It began with us noticing each other trudging up those wide stone stairs towards our two apartments, a circumstance which graduated to the exchange of friendly grins and sighs until, one Sunday afternoon, words were added—English words to start with (he noticed me carrying my newly-bought *Observer),* sporadic *svensk* phrases when, as time went on, the charts were being admired. We liked each other, I'll bluntly claim, a pure liking. Bo is mentioned often ("the nonagenarian Herr Bergman") in Michael Meyer's *Strindberg*, referred to in the 'Literary Biography' section above.*

And lastly, another Bergman. Not Ingrid, although I...no, that's another story, and totally commonplace. I mean Ingmar. I arrived in Stockholm in October and within one week of that arrival a small revue-cinema in the heart of town, the Bostock, began showing a complete season of the early films of Ingmar Bergman; these were the 'early' films because it was still early in Bergman's career, he was a young man still, in his thirties, only ten years older than I was. Anyhow by pure luck I attended the first evening of that season, and saw them all: titles like *Sommaren Med Monika*, and *Frenzy* and *Sawdust and Tinsel*. My favourite movie, by any director anywhere, anytime, is Bergman's *Wild Strawberries*, which in Swedish is *Smültronstället*: literally, *The Place of Wild Strawberries*. I can't even write these words without warming towards the film, mostly for Victor Sjöström, that old ravaged intelligent face (Sjöström was primarily, all his life, a director, not an actor, but Bergman's eye obviously told him something important in that regard); and, narrowing down the 'love', if that's what it is, of my vision, it's chiefly for the scene where the old professor, wandering around his childhood summer home, which he has not seen for many years, watches in his imagination the random group of children, all dressed in white, who are fishing or variously sitting or lying about on a grassy bank by the water, and sees also himself, an adolescent, as he falls irretrievably in love with a girl he'll somehow fail to marry. What does Proust say? (I mean, of course, what does he write?). "The true paradises are the ones we have lost." Sjöström's old iron face doesn't crumble as he watches that scene, but it's a near thing.

All this is so delicate and so fragrant with longing for a lost past it could have been written by Nabokov, it could be a scene from *Ada*, for instance, or from that beautiful memoir *Speak, Memory*. In the background of the Professor's overpowering memories during this journey (he's being driven from Stockholm down to the university

---

*I didn't even know Bo had reviewed plays until Meyer's book came along, and Bo probably knew very little of me (what was there to know? I was 27 years old). Truth is neither of us spoke the other's language easily. But we both did our best.

town of Lund, where he'll be given an honorary degree) are three young hitchhikers, one of whom is the young Bibi Andersson; Bergman and she were lovers during the shooting of this film (he was usually the lover of his leading ladies) and the camera does everything but acknowledge this, it leaves that glowing face only when there would be no more secrets to tell about their relationship if it stayed longer.

(For a month or two, one year, I was deliberating *hard* as to the possibility of Bergman ever needing a North American-type person of about my height and inarticulateness for some undefined purpose on the set, in any of his films, gofering, helping Sven Nyquist push a camera, whatever. I'd accidentally met, through a mutual friend, one of his 'actors' (actresses), Gertrud Fridh, a 30-second meeting, didn't really know her at all, but was weighing the odds. If I called, would Gertrud Fridh remember any of those thirty seconds? Something must have intervened to forestall my trying, I escaped embarrassing myself.)

13. Dr. Hammarskjöld and Alice

AT ONE POINT, about late May this was, just when he'd been complimenting himself on having lasted out the whole dark winter in a coldwater flat at the top of an old, since-demolished house in that quarter of the city called Klara, he noticed he was feeling kind of tiredish, which was a novel feeling for him, and a relative of the *arkitekt* who owned the flat recommended to him a GP named Hammarskjöld, first name now forgotten. The GP, who was a first cousin of the then-U.N. Secretary Dag Hammarskjöld, who's surely by miles the best and maybe the only *good* Secretary the U.N. has ever had, diagnosed incipient pneumonia, accused him of burning the candle at both ends, laughed quite a bit at this sally, and told him he was booking him into a hospital for a thorough check-up. Shortly afterwards he found himself in the Karolinska Institut, which he later learned was one of the world's leading teaching-hospitals. His room was on the ground floor of the hospital and had, in addition to its usual entrance from a hospital corridor, a door leading out into a courtyard. Within minutes of getting into the hospital gown and then into bed he was feeling entirely normal and natural but the head nurse of the section came in and took down an account of his past medical history, which was short and uncomplicated, and when that was over told him that her birthday was identical with his, only had occurred a few years earlier than his. There was no physical examination or testing that evening, that would come the next day, the head nurse said. After a time he was served dinner on a tray, none of which he cared for, and most of it went back to the kitchen. He wasn't at all tired now and the night took a long time getting started, what with corridor noise and so on, and it was some while after this that a night nurse came in, a cheerful buxom person named Alice Fägerström, who told him that she was, in spite of her Swedish name, a Finn, and explained that Finland had in fact two cultures, one of which spoke Finnish and the other, comprising one-third of the population, spoke Swedish. Alice sat on the edge of his bed during their chat. About eleven or so she asked if he was hungry and he admitted that he was, that he hadn't liked the dinner they'd provided. Alice agreed vehemently with this, the meals were terrible, she said. They were worse than that, they were *hemsk*, she said, which means ghastly. She then said she was going out to get him something decent. He didn't understand what she meant, he thought she'd simply go down the corridor to the cafeteria in the hospital and bring another tray back, but in fact she left the hospital, crossed a main road to one of the area's best restaurants, and had them make him a roast beef sandwich which must have had three portions of prime rib in it. It took her quite a while, of course, and he dozed off while he was waiting for her, so that when she got back she wasn't sure what to do but then she tidied up his sheet a little bit, she said, because she didn't want the roast beef to get cold, but it was fine, the tidying woke him up and the roast beef was not cold at all. He ate it while she sat on the bed and told him about the Russian invasion of Finland in 1941 and how the Finnish soldiers in their all-white uniforms had been invisible against the snowy mountains and had driven the numerically a hundred times bigger Red Army back towards Leningrad, slaughtering thousands of them. Sometime about three or 3.30 in the morning Alice had to go off and not long after that, when the Swedish midsummer night was already lightening, he found his clothes in an *armoire* at the back of the room and put them on and let himself out through the courtyard door. He never went back to the Karolinska Institut and never heard from them, either. As for Dr.Hammarskjöld, he never seemed in need of medical advice again during the time he spent in Sweden.

14.

THERE'S AN AWFUL LOT of the mythology of Sweden in those just-above paragraphs. And it's all so basic! But my heart bends a little when I think of it.

15.

SOMETIME SOON I have to mention the painting, the *capolavoro*, masterpiece, that established itself forever and ever, it now seems safe to say, inside my head during that much-abused Fifties decade. And pat on its cue, here it comes, my *capolavoro*, borne along in the wake of another unignorable topic. Which is, here's an unexpected presence in the queue, tennis.

Lawn tennis, as it insisted on being called back there in Cambridge.

Connolly, just quoted, writes,"I have loved poetry all my life". Time to come clean: I have not loved poetry all my life. Tennis, now, lawn or otherwise, that's a different matter. I began lobbing balls across or into the net about age six, with my father, who had been an outstanding player but who didn't lob enough balls at me when I was little to enable me to become even half as good as he must have been; but never mind that, the thing is that except for ten years from my middle 20s to middle 30s (i.e. my best years, what else) when my life was just too vagrant and unsettled to allow for anything like a racquet among my very light luggage, I have played tennis or played at it ever since.

(The American poet Galway Kinnell, in an interview, has said that many poets—he listed Roethke and Updike, among others—played and loved tennis, and Kinnell offered a possible explanation for this. The diagrammatic nature of the tennis court, with its clean straight lines and its insistent patterns, he theorized, resembles poetry in its formulaic aspect, line-and-stanza-lengths, rhyme schemes, etc. This seems to me pretty laborious but then again, on a long-shot basis, faintly tenable. Kinnell's listing of Updike here, however, a master prose-writer of our time whose published poetry has all the muscularity of a marshmallow, is pushing things a bit, but...no worries.)

And this connects to my *capolavoro* how?

Like this. In my final year at Cambridge University two things happened. I applied for a grant which my tutor had told me I'd have a decent chance for, a grant which would allow its recipient to spend a full year in Italy. The London committee then gave me a date on which I must appear before them to argue my case. Trouble was, one of my Cambridge finals was scheduled for that same morning and when I wrote to advise them of this and to ask for another date, I had by reply only the curtest of notes telling me that no rescheduling was possible. I would be judged, the note said, solely on my written application.

This sounded to me like a rejection and I don't think I'd have gone any further with it, that would have been *finis* for Italy and me, but during my next tutorial I happened to mention it to my tutor, a Mr. Potts (he could have been a character in an H.G. Wells novel, if only because of his red beard, his everpresent bicycle clips, and his name). Mr. Potts at once showed more energy than I'd seen in him all year. "We'll see about that", he muttered, and fired off a cable to that committee which must have singed its collective eyeballs. *At least* its eyeballs. A few days later I received from them, not a new date for an interview but the news that I had been awarded this year's grant, *sans* interview, *sans* a meeting of any sort. I never did see anybody face to face in this matter, only was sent, for starters, a modest cheque to cover the first month's R-&-B plus my one-way train ticket. Also the committee's unanimous good wishes for my year in what their letter, still preserved, calls *la bella Italia*.

I made a quick date with an Italian tutor in Cambridge, met him daily for sessions designed to give me some rudimentary phrases for my first weeks in his homeland, sessions during which, *very* oddly, we read aloud to each other cantos of Dante's *Divina Commedia* (this was equivalent, almost, to trying to learn English by reading Chaucer). I then headed off for *la bella* place.

Where tennis comes in is right here. In Cambridge I had been a member of the University Lawn Tennis Club, a privilege which you have to earn (you earn it by going at least a few rounds in the freshman tournament, under the scrutiny of two demi-gods, the ULTC Captain and the ULTC Secretary; I actually lost in the first round of that tournament, but in three sets, the only three-setter he was forced to play, to the eventual winner, a lanky fellow who'd been Eton champion the year before and whose name I still, with only an average amount of rancour, remember: *Andrew Kimpton, after half a century, what's up? have you been as lucky in life as you were against me?*) and which allows you free lessons from a very good coach (ours, a Mr. Smith, was flown to the U.S. every summer to coach, on service alone, the American Junior Davis Cup team) plus a chance at a Half-Blue if you are picked to play for the big team in the Oxford match (I was not so picked...long story). I had however played in numerous other of our pre-Oxford matches as a member of the Grasshoppers, the Light Blue's second six, as it were, and on that basis had spent two days on the courts of the Queen's Club in London, next door to Wimbledon; the same two days, it turned out, which a number of American players had booked for their pre-Wimbledon grasscourt workouts. On one of those days we had a match with them, not us vs. them, needless to say, but a mock-match in which one Grasshopper got to partner one big-time American against two similarly-selected players. I cannot remember who my partner for this one-set match was (although it could have been, probably wasn't or I'd remember him, Tony Trabert, who was heading up the U.S.contingent; Vic Seixas?...nothing stirs), but I know that Maureen Connolly, then the world's no.1 woman player, was on the other side of the net.

An unearned brush with fame, for sure. A sad brush, in that this was, I think, the last year of Maureen Connolly's career: she was injured in a riding accident in California a few months later.

(One more sentimental salute to tennis while I'm at it. Living for a month one springtime in London House, a hostel near Mecklenburgh Square reserved in those years for Commonwealth students, I played tennis a half-dozen mornings in a nearby park in the square, and my playing-partner and I began to notice, the second or third of those mornings, a well-built blonde in a pale blue probably-cashmere V-neck who would walk into the park from a house on the square and hang about the court for a bit, obviously attracted by our cannon-ball serves, pin-point volleying, etc. This, we learned after consultation with the porter back at LH, was Diana Dors. Early-model DD.

That's all. She'd amble back into her house again before we'd settled anything.)

I'm taking a long while to get to my tale of a *capolavoro*.

We now return to it, speeding up as we go. One of my mates at the University club in Cambridge was a young Italian, Guido-some-thing, a native of Florence, surname now sunk irretrievably beneath the waves. Adriatic waves, Mediterranean waves, Ligurian waves, one or more of those. When I arrived in Italy and had taken a peek at Pavia, the town my grant recommended I spend my time in*, and secondly at Rome, where a sordid episode on a street just behind the Via Veneto persuaded me not to loiter, I entrained for Florence, fell in love with the high cobalt sky outside the train station in about one milli-second, found almost as quickly a very large room in a house once inhabited by Machiavelli, located Guido and played tennis with him on a red-clay court surrounded by cypress trees (I still remember the warm sun of that day and the red clay and the blue sky and the near-overwhelming sense I had of doing this thing that I was so fond of doing, i.e. hitting a tennis ball back and forth over a net, in this historically-breathtaking place)…and a few days later went to Guido's home for lunch. Which is where the plot at last shows itself for what it is.

Which is: an infatuation and a falling-in-love.

The first was with Guido's mother.

Calma, calma, it's not what you think.

It was just the three of us for lunch. The signora was a scholar, I've forgotten what her discipline was, and was perhaps 46 or 47 years old. She spoke excellent English, which meant that I seldom got to amuse my two lunch-companions with my 15th-century Italian vocabulary and my antique Dantesque accent. She was also (sorry to

---

*The peek was enough.

keep mentioning this sort of thing, I mean the ravishing good looks of almost every woman who makes it into these pages) (up to you to decide how you feel about this) handsome in a way that seemed to me more taken-for-granted by herself and family than it merited being. She was grave in bearing and voice and her dark hair was very faintly graying. It's the gravity that could normally be counted on to impress me. I would gladly have heard her voice more often than I did, which usually consisted in all-too-brief exchanges after or before my two or three sets with Guido. On this first occasion, though, she spoke at length of her city, which she loved, and occasionally left us alone at the table while she sought out a book or a photograph to show me. She also asked me what I had seen and not seen, suggested walks which she herself often took and would never, she thought, tire of, advised me to visit two, in particular, of the nearby hill-towns, and wrote out for me the address of a friend in Siena whom I must visit for a weekend in order to study the works of Siena's most celebrated painter, Duccio di Buoninsegna, locally and generally 'Duccio'. A painter renowned for his *gentilezza*, I remember her saying.

And then it came—

The falling-in-love.

With a painting. A painting by a Florentine painter named Massacio. A painting, a fresco to be exact, called *The Expulsion from the Garden*.

There was, not far from here, the signora told me—and no, she would not show me a book or a print of anything by this man, she said, I would see what he could do without any diminishing warnings or preparations from either book or print—a church, the church of Santa Maria del Carmine. In the Santa Maria del Carmine was a chapel, the Cappella Brancacci; and in this chapel were…what I must see. If I never entered the Uffizi, if the Boboli gardens remained nothing more than a north-of-town myth, if I never walked down the vast grey length of the Duomo or mused before Ghiberti's bronze doors, it would be small loss compared to the crime against my own eyes of which I would be guilty if I failed to see Masaccio's frescoes. Especially one of them, one above all, above anything I would see in her town, in Tuscany, in, it was possible, her country. Guido was rolling his eyes behind her back, he was distancing himself from this adoration, he was apologizing for this uncool un-Florentine behaviour on his mother's part. *Basta già*, enough already, he was signalling....

Enough of this preamble, too. The next morning I was there, at the Santa Maria del Carmine. About the middle of the morning, ten or eleven it must have been. The whole place was in darkness. The street-door opened when I tried it...darkness. I entered anyway, walked a few steps, I had to feel my way against a wall. I called out. Nothing. Called again. A minute or so later there was an answer, there was then a small moving light in a side-aisle, and a man appeared. A janitor, overalled, with a flashlight. I explained, omitting the 15th-century Dante routine, using a few words in English, naming the name. Ah, he said, Masaccio, *si, si*. The signore wishes to see the Masaccios? *Si, si, bene, benissimmo.*

He left me for a short while, some lights went on, he returned, gestured, smiled, I heard the word '*solo*'. This I could, I hoped, understand: he would leave me alone, fine. He walked briskly off. And there I was with the frescoes.

Not to be too long about this: there were several fresckes, at least one of them, I later learned, probably not by the master, probably by 'the school of', the best known of these called 'The Rendering of the Tribute Money'. None of them had half the interest, to me, of almost any of the walls in the Uffizi, walls I *had* seen, across town from where I now stood.

But then there was the 'Expulsion'. Adam and Eve, overcome by the enormity of what was happening to them, a sword-carrying angel overhead, the angel clad in gold fire and pointing them where they must now go, both of them naked, shielding their nakednesses, covering their eyes, Eve's lifted mouth a black hole, every gesture brimming with catastrophe—

I sat and watched them, they seemed to move. The angel was hurrying them from above, hurrying or harrying them out of Eden, but a heavy beauty was slowing their movements, they were suffocating in it—

A while went by. The janitor looked in and went off again. I walked about, stood near, stood further off. When events began to repeat themselves, when the same thoughts returned for the second or third time, it seemed permissible to leave. *Basta per oggi*, I told myself.

Enough for today. I could manage the simple sentence, and it's what I said, muttered, murmured, however it sounded to him, to the janitor, thanking him for the light. He showed me where the light-switch was, "if the signore wishes to come again". I guessed I would wish, and thanked him again. And left.

Yes, I went back fairly often during those next seven months, nine or ten times perhaps. I was living not far off, via de' Bardi, the same street that George Eliot's Romola lived on, a ten-minute walk—and almost every time that I went there to sit before our primaeval parents I was on my own. Nobody else around. The janitor approved of my taste: he didn't think much of *The Tribute Money* either. I never spoke of it again with the signora, Guido's mother. Didn't go on playing much tennis, either, other things began happening. I was trying to justify my grant, I was there to write, writing was getting itself done, much too tortuous to be of interest, ultimately, to anyone but myself but, you know, those inflated sentences have to be shaken out of the system sooner or later, never mind how unuseable they'll look eventually. All that laborious making and remaking and un-making!....

So it was. I still keep the best reproduction of Masaccio's *Expulsion from the Garden* that money can buy on my workroom wall. It still matters as much to me as any other single painting I have seen. Its only rivals, if that's the word (and it isn't: there's no rivalry here, just several different experiences of almost uniquely deep sensations), are a few Edvard Munch paintings and a few of Caspar David Friedrich's—I have an uncomplicated taste, sentimentality dripping from practically all of its frames, can't be helped—and, who else, the Shakespeare of painting, Rembrandt.

A *reminder* is all that my repro-*Expulsion* is, of course, not a piece of art. Still.

Twenty-some years ago, about 1985 or 6, my family and I were in Florence and we walked from our hotel to the Santa Maria del Carmine with varying degrees of anticipation, family having heard quite enough already about this waiting event, this patient vision, thanks a lot, but willing to donate the morning to it, everybody gamely up for it. Nobody rolling their eyes as Guido had done. I'm pretty sure they weren't doing that. We found a queue of forty or fifty people standing outside the church, nothing compared to the thousand or two outside the Uffizi of course, but a shock nonetheless, a blow to at least one of those taking up his position at the back of the queue. There were the usual gallery-type velvet ropes to keep us in order when, having paid our entrance fees, we'd finally got inside. A TV-crew were just setting up, though I think they were going to do *The Tribute Money*.

Pretty interesting, somebody said as we left. And it was, too. *Molto* interesting is what it was. Compared to what it had been when I'd had to ask for a light to be switched on in there.

Those unlit Fifties!

16.

Altri episòdi italiani

In Italy I discovered Giacomo Leopardi. You cannot be more 'romantic' than Leopardi, and there are times when it suffocates, that wispy voice, like Rilke's; Rilke who at his best astonishes the mind and the heart and leaves them, for a while, as 'new' as hardly anyone else in the world has ever managed to do—but who at his worst is hardly bearable in his tremulous delicacy. But out of such often-frail pages come, from Leopardi, also these three lines:

Canti, e così trapassi / Dell'anno e di tua vita / il più bel fiore.

which is, in my own uncomplicated translation,

You sing, and so passes / the loveliest flower of the year / and of your life.

—and for this I am ready to say, and, as you have seen and are now about to see again, to write, the line Cyril Connolly wrote which is quoted somewhere above: "For me to love the poem is to love the poet who wrote it and become his man". There is surely nothing, not a syllable, in these three Leopardi lines, which brings anything new into the world or into the reader's mind, it is a compilation of tritenesses —and yet its swift load of heart-scouring power is irresistible. You read it and you think: *That is so. I cannot prevent this or alter it.* Or you think, even more harshly, desolately: *That is so. It has already passed by, my song.* A dying woman friend of Henry James wrote to him, near death, this: "You must tell me something that you are sure is true". James failed to do this, he recoiled from the cry, it's not clear whether he really recognized its nakedness, whether he understood his dying friend's final impatience with most words. And who's to blame him? But I do blame him. I blame him for doing neither of these two things: travelling to her and taking her in his arms (the idea would have unsettled and alarmed him), or, best of all, writing to her to say, *Nobody before you has ever written that line.*

17.

TWO SENTENCES from Joyce's friend Italo Svevo, in his novel *Confessions of Zeno*: "I am getting old and it is some time now since women ceased to take any interest in me. If I were to lose interest in them, there would be an end to all relationship between us."

18.

The sculptured figures in the *Capella Medici*, the Medici Chapel, in Florence. Those two brothers, Giuliano and Lorenzo, loll in their robes, larger than life and controlling, languidly but terribly, all the white marble in the room. You know, watching them, that they are still dangerous.

And beside them, four nude figures, most arrestingly the female figures of Twilight and Night, those long asexual bodies, pondering how to use the immense limbs they have been given.

19.

An incident during the *Maggio Musicale*, the Musical May, which is a Florentine festival of, primarily, operas. This was a performance of Verdi's *Otello*, and I was seated on the long curved stone bench in the top gallery among the *cittadini*, not down below with the local aristocracy and the (largely American, in those days) tourists. Renata Tebaldi's Desdemona was playing opposite Ramon Vinay, the Spanish tenor. Vinay was in poor voice, poor health, it soon became clear: he couldn't hit his high notes, he couldn't *hold* any kind of note, and the whistles soon began, and grew, and crescendoed. He gestured, pointed to his throat, he was practically mouthing the word laryngitis. The galleryites were not appeased, the cushions began to fly. They drove him out of the performance that night. After the interval a substitute appeared, unhappily a short man for whom it appeared no costume had been budgeted, and the much taller Vinay's robes were too long, they dragged on the stage floor when the mock-Otello moved. The crowd reviled him for being second-rate, for being short, for polishing the stage-floor with his unmanageable trailing costume. A group off to my right organized a chant listing the names of taller tenors with whom they were even now in negotiation. Tebaldi, all this time, whenever she appeared, was applauded to the rafters (in the absence of rafters, applauded to the thousands of darkened, patiently waiting ceiling-bulbs). When the performance ended no one came out from behind the curtain, nothing moved on the curtained stage. The crowd, which had always, it was clear, adored Tebaldi, wanted her, they cried out her name, they chanted it in something very close to unison, over and over, they could have been a well-rehearsed chorus. Finally, finally, she came. They were ecstatic, they rose to their feet, flowers were brought up on stage, the chants of *Renata, Renata* and *Tebaldi, Tebaldi* were endless She stood there, she threw the bouquets onto the stage-floor at each side of her, she looked at her adorers and swept her hand in a gesture we all understood, a universally-recognized gesture of contempt, of derision. Her fury burned outwards over the rows and rows of now-silent opera-goers, over the bejeweled ones closest to her but reaching to the rest of us higher up too, she meanwhile motionless, not a tremor to mar the contempt etched on her face. One last look, to make sure her gaze had scarred its way even unto the farthest reaches of the house, to be satisfied that it had been seen and understood everywhere, by everyone, and she turned and strode off. *Canaille,* one could almost hear her saying: *treat my Otello, my Ramon, my companions, in that fashion, will you? You will not soon see me again.* I know that it was the last of her performances that May. It may have been the last time the Florentine *Maggio Musicale* ever saw or heard her.

20.

FINAL FIRENZE MEMORY, for me the most intimate. I had been strolling about the town that morning and had ended up on the crenellated roof-deck of the Palazzo Vecchio, the old City Hall, overlooking the town. Standing there I'd fallen into conversation with an American of about my age; he was newly arrived, I was a veritable fount of information regarding what lay below us. We decided to lunch together and I led the way to the Trattoria Camillo, a family-run place on Via Santo Spirito, very near my rooms on the via de' Bardi. I'd been there a few times without anything noteworthy having taken place, just good food at a price a grantee like me could afford. We took our places and ordered our *antipasti*. Waiting for it to arrive I suddenly remembered I didn't have a lot of lire in my wallet; I took the wallet from my back pocket and had a surreptitious look. Right, *merde*, I had barely enough to pay for what I'd just ordered. Not a good discovery, sitting there with somebody I hardly knew, not good at all, but so far I could cover it. I was sure nobody had noticed any of this, people had been walking about and the place was busy. *Antipasti* gone, the signora arrived to take our next orders. My companion ordered a pasta and a glass of red wine, I said I was fine, not hungry, a carafe of water, nothing more, *grazie*. I half-thought the signora gave me a second look, but I wasn't sure and I didn't keep thinking it. She left, was back again in minutes with not one but two plates of pasta and two glasses of *chianti*. I shook my head, said I'd ordered neither of these, she seemed too busy to listen and went off. I pondered this but after she'd gone determinedly past our table a couple of times without looking, I ate my pasta and enjoyed my wine. The pasta would soon have cooled past its best, after all. The American then ordered a salad, I again declined, again two orders arrived. By then I had given up. Lunch ended with two desserts, I don't remember what these were, chocolate cake was what I normally liked and still do like along with red wine; and *due cappuccini*.

We'd finished. I asked for our bills, they arrived. I got a quick look at his, it was in order, everything he'd had was listed. My bill was for that initial *antipàsto*. Nothing more than that, nothing after that. The signora, in passing, gave me a quick look when we were on our way out and paying the grandmother who presided over the till. She didn't wink, but she looked. It was a placid, friendly, everyday sort of look. The American had noticed nothing. He and I shook hands and parted as we left and didn't meet again.

I went back to Camillo's a few days later and left a tip which covered my share of that meal. The signora may have noticed this, may not. My guess is that she did but there was no way of knowing. I have no memory of nodding or smiling or giving her a small bow or a meaningful, as they say, glance. Camillo's still exists but it's gone gourmet, it caters to the monied classes and has a half-dozen waiters in white livery. The family has clearly exited the premises, I hope with their pockets stuffed. I hope that the signora, who can hardly still be of this world, had as calmly assured and sharp-eyed and generous (and perhaps, trusting) a series of days until her days ended.

Northern Ireland, 1954.

Seminar at York University, ca. 1970.
Photo by Michael Levanbaum

Acknowledgements

My thanks to numerous advisors, especially my family, on matters ranging from themes to headings to ruminations of a general sort. Also to my editor, Carmine Starnino, who suggested this book; the swiftness of understanding between us was something I would wish every writer. And to my publisher, Simon Dardick: courtesy incarnate.

Signal
EDITIONS

Carmine Starnino, Editor
Michael Harris, Founding Editor

WRESTLING WITH ANGELS: SELECTED POEMS Doug Beardsley
HIDE & SEEK Susan Glickman
MAPPING THE CHAOS Rhea Tregebov
FIRE NEVER SLEEPS Carla Hartsfield
THE RHINO GATE POEMS George Ellenbogen
SHADOW CABINET Richard Sanger
MAP OF DREAMS Ricardo Sternberg
THE NEW WORLD Carmine Starnino
THE LONG COLD GREEN EVENINGS OF SPRING Elisabeth Harvor
FAULT LINE Laura Lush
WHITE STONE: THE ALICE POEMS Stephanie Bolster
KEEP IT ALL Yves Boisvert (Translated by Judith Cowan)
THE GREEN ALEMBIC Louise Fabiani
THE ISLAND IN WINTER Terence Young
A TINKERS' PICNIC Peter Richardson
SARACEN ISLAND: THE POEMS OF ANDREAS KARAVIS David Solway
BEAUTIES ON MAD RIVER: SELECTED AND NEW POEMS Jan Conn
WIND AND ROOT Brent MacLaine
HISTORIES Andrew Steinmetz
ARABY Eric Ormsby
WORDS THAT WALK IN THE NIGHT Pierre Morency
    (Translated by Lissa Cowan and René Brisebois)
A PICNIC ON ICE: SELECTED POEMS Matthew Sweeney
HELIX: NEW AND SELECTED POEMS John Steffler
HERESIES: THE COMPLETE POEMS OF ANNE WILKINSON, 1924-1961
    Edited by Dean Irvine
CALLING HOME Richard Sanger
FIELDER'S CHOICE Elise Partridge
MERRYBEGOT Mary Dalton
MOUNTAIN TEA Peter Van Toorn
AN ABC OF BELLY WORK Peter Richardson
RUNNING IN PROSPECT CEMETERY Susan Glickman
MIRABEL Pierre Nepveu (Translated by Judith Cowan)
POSTSCRIPT Geoffrey Cook
STANDING WAVE Robert Allen
THERE, THERE Patrick Warner
HOW WE ALL SWIFTLY: THE FIRST SIX BOOKS Don Coles
THE NEW CANON: AN ANTHOLOGY OF CANADIAN POETRY
    Edited by Carmine Starnino
OUT TO DRY IN CAPE BRETON Anita Lahey
RED LEDGER Mary Dalton
REACHING FOR CLEAR David Solway
OX Christopher Patton
A DROPPED GLOVE IN REGENT STREET: AN AUTOBIOGRAPHY
    BY OTHER MEANS Don Coles

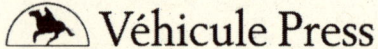 Véhicule Press